REVIVAL People

REVIVAL People

Nico Smit

Copyright © 2025 by Nico Smit
Nico Smit's blog: nicosmitblog.com

First published by Yeshua Collective 2025
All rights reserved. No part of this book may be reproduced in any manner whatsoever without written permission except in the case of brief quotations embodied in critical articles and reviews.

Unless otherwise noted, all Scripture quotations taken from The Holy Bible, New International Version® NIV®
Copyright © 1973, 1978, 1984, 2011 by Biblica, Inc.
Used with permission. All rights reserved worldwide.

Scriptures marked CEV are taken from the CONTEMPORARY ENGLISH VERSION (CEV): Scripture taken from the CONTEMPORARY ENGLISH VERSION copyright© 1995 by the American Bible Society. Used by permission.

Scriptures marked NLT are taken from the HOLY BIBLE, NEW LIVING TRANSLATION (NLT): Scriptures taken from the HOLY BIBLE, NEW LIVING TRANSLATION, Copyright© 1996, 2004, 2007 by Tyndale House Foundation. Used by permission of Tyndale House Publishers, Inc., Carol Stream, Illinois 60188. All rights reserved. Used by permission.

Scriptures marked KJV are taken from the KING JAMES VERSION (KJV): KING JAMES VERSION, public domain.

First Printing, 2025 by Ingram Spark
ISBN (print book): 978-1-7635476-7-4
ISBN (ebook): 978-1-7635476-8-1

Published by Yeshua Collective
58 Channel Highway, Kingston TAS 7050
PO Box 329, Kingston TAS 7051

yeshuacollective.com

Cover design by Matthew de Livera, @mdfilmcreative
Edited by BekkerMedia, New South Wales, Australia
www.bekkermedia.com

CONTENTS

ENDORSEMENTS vii
FOREWORD xiii
PROLOGUE xvii

- Introduction: Revival Is An Invitation — 1
1. The Fears People Have About Revival — 9
2. The Pre-Revival Battle — 23
3. A Move Of Restoration — 35
4. Demanding More — 45
5. Let Your Love Spark a Revival — 51
6. Intimacy Has Side-Effects — 59
7. Don't Be Caught Asleep! — 65
8. The Dress Rehearsal — 75
9. Revival Is Costly But Affordable — 83
10. Pentecost Is For Everyone — 93
11. Conclusion: Revival Is Waiting For You — 101

ENDORSEMENTS

I say a big 'Amen' to the prophetic and stirring call of Pastor Nico's new book, *REVIVAL People.* I love the heart behind this book because you can quickly discern that the author has personally never graduated from living hungry and thirsty for the Holy Spirit. And as a result of reading these pages, you will receive an impartation of burning zeal to live as an authentic Book-of-Acts Christ-follower. After all, as Pastor Nico observes, we don't need to cry out for 'another Pentecost.' Instead, we need to live like the Day of Pentecost outpouring that took place 2,000 years ago is a real and relevant experience in our lives today.

Larry Sparks, Texas, USA
Publisher, Author, TV host, International Speaker and Preacher
Publisher at Destiny Image
Serves on Apostolic Council of Prophetic Elders (ACPE)
larrysparksministries.com

Every Generation has a witness. When Jesus told His disciples to wait in Jerusalem until they were imbued with power, it was so that they would become "witnesses". God anoints people in every generation as witnesses of the resurrection of Jesus Christ. In the midst of witnesses God raises up voices, champions of His cause in the nations of the earth. Pastors Nico and Joe-Ann Smit are just that - serial church planters and revivalists who have given their lives to the equipping of God's people in His Great Harvest of souls. True soul winners and shepherds themselves, Pastors Nico and Joe-Ann are champions of the local church and the global body of Christ.

I am grateful Pastor Nico wrote this book. Having been his friend for a few years now, I admire his heart for people and his stand for truth.

REVIVAL People will challenge complacency, demonstrate that there is more to be pursued in revival amongst a local church people, and send laborers into the harvest like never before. As Pastor Nico says, "Revival does not live in buildings, but in people." I pray you become a Revival PERSON as you enjoy this read and receive its impartation TODAY - in JESUS NAME!

Kris Kildosher, Omaha NE, USA
Revivalist, Traveling Missionary, Preacher, Church Planter and Ministry School Founder
Kris Kildosher Ministries - kriskildosher.com
Activate School of the Spirit

I'm delighted to tell you to read the book *REVIVAL People* by my dear friend, Nico Smit. He's a man of God on fire with revival in the Southern parts of Australia. I have been there and have seen God move there. This book is not just about living in revival on a Sunday but living in revival every day. It is about putting your roots deep into the river of God's presence, not just for a moment but for your whole entire life. We can live it in the workplace, we can live it in the church, we can live it everywhere! Why not? We certainly should.

Get this book, get equipped to live in the river of God's presence daily and take the Gospel across the nations. God bless you as you read it.

Ben Fitzgerald, Germany
Revivalist, Preacher, Church Planter and Evangelism Mobilizer
Senior leader of Awakening Europe and Awakening Australia

REVIVAL People by Pastor Nico Smit is a call to awaken a passion for revival in both the local church and the world. Pastor Nico's ministry inspires me greatly. His heart for revival is impacting many in Australia in a powerful way.

REVIVAL People is more than just another book; it's a rallying cry for those longing for Holy Ghost revival. Thank you, Pastor Nico, for challenging the church to believe God to touch the world again with revival!

David Hall, Adelaide, Australia
Revivalist, Pastor and Conference Speaker, Senior Pastor at Revival City Church
State President, Australian Christian Churches (Assemblies of God), South Australia

In today's charismatic movement of churches, the term 'revival' can be loosely tossed around in obscure and sometimes unapproachable ways. *REVIVAL People* takes this topic and dives directly into the deep end of it, allowing the reader to get honest and practical with how they live out the tangible love of Jesus in their personal and corporate lives.

This book is truly amazing! Nico is a father who truly walks out what he preaches. The book you are holding is profoundly practical and approachable for anyone reading it. He raises real questions and meets the reader with answers in a way that is sure to inspire and challenge how we operate. This book isn't simply for better church meetings, it's a call to find the Lord all around us and walk into a Jesus people revival.

Way to go!!! This will be a gift for the body!!! It's stunning.

Peter Mattis, Redding CA, USA
Pastor, Teacher, Worship Leader and Songwriter, Worship Pastor of Bethel Church

"He who has an ear to hear what the spirit of the Lord is saying!"

REVIVAL People is what the Spirit of the Lord is saying in this hour to His people. This book is filled with strategy and instruction for all those who are TRULY in pursuit of revival! It is for those who are truly crying out like the psalmist, *"Will you not revive us again oh Lord that we may rejoice in you!"*

The passion with which the words in these chapters are penned, will invoke the reader to be ignited with the fire of pursuit.

The "one line" encapsulations of divine instruction abundantly woven throughout this book jolts one to reset for a pursuit that is altogether pure by exposing the vanity of futile pursuits in modern day church culture; pursuits that don't bring forth the fruits of the dominion of the kingdom.

It's time for a reset in the church. *REVIVAL People* is the manual to bring the church into this alignment.

Anita Alexander, Gold Coast QLD, Australia

Prophetic Revivalist, Teacher, Intercessor, Psalmist, Author, and Songwriter, Co-founder and Pastor of Golden City Church

Overseer of Kingdom Academy School of the Spirit, Director of Revival Flame Ministries - revival-flame.org

Member of the Australian Prophetic Council

In this book Pastor Nico Smit skillfully navigates his readers on a journey full of insights on the subject of revival which has been his passion for over 30 years. The book is well researched, factual, educational and relevant for our times. This book is designed to open the eyes of your understanding and equip you, step by step, to trigger revival in our times.

I fully agree with the author that revival is an invitation to encounter God's presence in the way that changes everything. Revival does not live in buildings, but in people, hungry people, praying people, obedient people and repenting people.

This is a must-read book for those who are not satisfied with the normal. It will capture the spirit of a man who believes revival is God's answer to a broken and weary world.

My prayer is that *REVIVAL People* will be used as a great instrument of God for ushering unprecedented revival in these last days.

Joe Imakando, Lusaka, Zambia
Bishop, Teacher, Author, Conference Speaker and Broadcaster
General Overseer Bread of Life Church International
Member of the African Apostolic Council

I have had the privilege of knowing Nico Smit as a fellow minister on the Australian Prophetic Council, and I can confidently say that he is not just someone who speaks about revival—he embodies it. His passion for awakening the Church to live in a continuous, Spirit-filled movement of God is unmistakable.

The truest manifestation of revival is not confined to a church service or a moment of emotional fervor—it is a life fully yielded to the presence and power of God. In *REVIVAL People* Nico beautifully articulates how revival must flow beyond the four walls of the Church and into the streets, workplaces, and everyday lives of believers. As you read this book, expect to be challenged, stirred, and equipped to become a carrier of revival in your world. This is a must-read for every believer, hungry for authentic Kingdom impact.

David Balestri, Sydney, Australia
Author, Prophetic Minister and Entrepreneur, Founder of Marketplace Invasion
Business pastor of multi-site church HopeUC
Member of the Australian Prophetic Council

FOREWORD

The greatest farmer the world has ever known is pursuing the greatest harvest the world has ever seen, through a family of sons and daughters - revival people full of power, love, and wisdom. We are living in a season when *"...the plowman will overtake the reaper, and the treader of grapes him who sows seed."* (Amos 9:13).

REVIVAL people are motivated by the mandate of the Great Commission and the Great Commandment. Jesus did not give us a commission and then leave us without the ability to fulfill it. He gave us the power of the Holy Spirit to enable and empower us to accomplish the Great Commission. He gave us the fire of love—the flame of the Holy Spirit—so we could fulfill the Great Commandment: to love God, ourselves, and the world with such passion that the world would believe who we are.

On the day of Pentecost, the disciples received the Holy Spirit in three forms: the wind, the fire, and the wine. The wind represents power, the fire symbolizes passion, and the wine embodies the pleasure of revival people.

In 1995, my life was transformed by the power, passion, and pleasure of the Holy Spirit. As a Baptist pastor in a dry season, I was hungry to experience more of God. Then, Dr. Randy Clark laid hands on me, released the river of revival, and I received an impartation along with a prophetic word. The fruit of that encounter has been 1.4 million names added to the Lamb's Book of Life, more than 300,000 healings, and the birth of a revival people in 22 nations. Sons and daughters of glory are now burning brightly without burning out—because they are like the wise virgins with oil in their lamps.

When I graduated with a doctoral degree, I felt the Holy Spirit whisper, "It is time to slow down enough to catch up with Jesus." It was an invitation to return to my first love. I had become so busy working for Him that I was no longer flowing from Him. Since then, I have been on a daily journey of personal revival—to be with Jesus, become like Jesus, and live and love like Him.

While ministering to a large group of people in Australia, I had the honor of meeting Pastor Nico Smit. When he shared his passion for revival people. The Holy Spirit began to move. I found myself becoming increasingly hungry for His presence.

Revival people are ordinary believers experiencing revival here and now. *REVIVAL People* is about habitation, not just visitation. Pastor Nico provides a blueprint and clear guidance on how to move in the flow of God's great plan.

After reading this book, I knew this was not just an invitation but an impartation—an opportunity to step into a revival that has been waiting for both you and me. One burning question remains after reading this book: How do you want to be remembered and on what side of history do you want to be a part of?

Pastor Nico invites us to follow Jesus to a well—to allow Him to deal with the waters we have been drinking from. Jesus offers us living water that satisfies our deepest longings. This pure, revival water—the river—is being released through you, in its fullness, leading to the greatest harvest the earth has ever known. It will be glorious.

Of the hundreds of books I have read about revival, this is one of the best. Read it slowly, and allow it to read you.

Dr. Leif Hetland, Atlanta GA, USA
Author, International Speaker and Preacher
Founder and president of Global Mission Awareness
Bestselling Author of 'Called To Reign' and 'The Love Awakening'

PROLOGUE

What do you think of when you hear the word, 'revival'?

In this book, we're going to forget everything we thought we knew about revival and deeply explore what God tells us revival actually is.

Any revival that can only show up at church on Sunday is not a true revival! A church in revival is always in revival. They don't need a pulpit to have a ministry or a purpose. They don't need a program or a run-sheet to make it happen. They don't need a special event so they can conjure something up. They don't need a building to prove they should exist. No, they get their fire from God, and they cannot hold it back. They are good news to the poor wherever and whenever they find them. And they are always looking!

Revival is God's answer to a broken, weary world. It is His refreshing water making glad the city, pouring out love to the orphans and bringing hope to the captives. God does not send revival so it can be confined within man's walls, limited by man's traditions or simply used so men can entertain themselves. Let's be honest with ourselves ... any revival that does not break through the walls of the church to flood the streets of the city with the love of God cannot truly be a move birthed in His heart and by His Spirit.

Many cry out for revival but have no ministry outside their buildings. This could be the problem. Revival does not live in buildings, but in people... hungry people... praying people... obedient people... repenting people... people who want to do what Jesus asked them! Revival is waiting for people to walk in it. Revival is waiting for worshippers to live out what God called them to do. This is why revival should never be defined as an event, an exception, a special service, a crusade or another Sunday service. When a Christian walks in revival they share the GOOD NEWS with MEGA JOY to ALL they see.

To the Christian it must be a way of life. When revival touches a church, it should awaken a giant, transform a culture, and move a nation. Anything less is to dam what God wants to overflow!

I have been passionate about this topic for over 30 years. I have lived it, I have pursued it and I have encouraged it for as long as I can remember. I was born-again in a revival and it is one of those 'once you've tasted it, you would not be satisfied with anything less' kind of things. I'm not talking about happy church meetings or even powerful crusades. Those are wonderful, but the revival I am so passionate about is one where the scent does not leave, the heart does not grow cold, and the power does not fade.

REVIVAL people are people who live with a daily expectation that revival is here!
It is not a 'what if', but rather a 'how can I' kind of book. We are not waiting for another Pentecost… we're pushing into God's promise of living out the resurrected life that is already awakened in us. Revival means to 'to live again'!

Revival is nothing more than saints returning to normal!
When people look at you, they should not say:
"O, what nice doctrine you have!",
"O, what a cool church you attend!",
"O, what awesome things you own!" or
"O, look how admired, popular and evolved you are!"

… NO… they should say: "WOW, there is the Gospel walking! I can see Jesus in you!"

That is the point of this book. Revival is nothing more than a people who are saturated with God! The Bible says: Jesus was made fully alive in the Spirit. (1 Peter 3:18) He came that we would be brought back to life! We are to LIVE in the breath of God that lives in us. We need revival for resurrection from sleep, we need the same Spirit that manifested in Jesus to manifest in us, and we need revival to stay FULLY alive in Christ.

We must be REVIVAL people. The church of Acts is known for one very significant thing...the HOLY SPIRIT is ALWAYS in attendance. They were a community of worshippers ignited by God with the fire of God. Pentecost was a once off event that opened the door and released God's flame so that nobody needed to ever live without a continuous revival. This is why revival should not only be an event, an exception, a special service or crusade. To the Christian it must be a way of life.

If revival is to live it must live in people. It must exist in intimacy, rise in the heart and overflow onto everything the Christian touches. It is not the product of better teaching, better facilities or greater skill, but the result of desperately hungry people wanting God ABOVE and BEFORE anything else! Revival is how God responds when hunger causes a person to reach out and touch His presence!

Nearly 120 years ago William Booth made this prophetic statement: "The chief danger of the 20th century will be having religion without the Holy Spirit, Christianity without Christ, forgiveness without repentance, salvation without regeneration, politics without God, and heaven without hell."

Any form of Christianity that tries to exist without the living Holy Spirit burning within it and bursting out of it, is dead and in need of revival. Any follower of Jesus who wants to do what Jesus did without the spiritual life He had, will fail. The fire in our bones, the blaze in our hearts, the 'GO' in our step and the power in our lives must be oiled by God, fired up by His Holy Spirit and designed to be the engine room of the supernatural life.

"Revival is nothing more than a new beginning to our first obedience to God's invitation." (Charles Grandison Finney (1835). "Lectures on Revivals of Religion", p.14.)

REVIVAL is the breath of God that inspires a person to live again. Consider the fact that every time a human being breathes out, they expire. In the natural a person expires on average 22,000 times a day. Unless another breath is given life will cease. Such is REVIVAL in the life of a Christian. We live by the breath gift of God. Without continuous REVIVAL the Christian can drift into a state of lifelessness, fruitlessness, joylessness and hopelessness.

Everybody is invited to be a REVIVAL person!

Pentecost is knowledge turned into experience! Having a theory of revival is very different than having the experience. There are many Christians who know what the Bible says, but because they have no experience, they struggle to make sense of it. The flames ON the heads of those in the upper room set fire to the knowledge IN their heads. This is a supernatural conversion that still turns information into practice. Many have prayed for years asking for an invitation to revival, but it is here…and it is available right now. The question is: will you drop everything and enter in? Will you give God permission to fill you with His fire? Or is the idea of it more appealing than the practice?

I pray as you read this book your expectations of the fullness of God in you will rise and you will truly see yourself as a REVIVAL person!

Introduction: Revival Is An Invitation

Revival is not a fleeting moment. It's not a weekend event or a once-in-a-lifetime experience. Revival is an invitation from God to awaken what is dormant, to revive what has grown cold, and to bring life to what has nearly expired. It is not something we personally orchestrate but something we respond to. Without the Holy Spirit, Christianity loses its vitality—it becomes a lifeless shell of rituals and traditions. It is the Spirit who breathes life into our faith and keeps us burning with passion for God. Revival is never forced. It is always an invitation, extended in love, to those who will come.

To revive means 'to live again'. It is God's answer to spiritual exhaustion and complacency. Pentecost was the doorway to a life of continual revival. When the Holy Spirit descended like tongues of fire, He didn't come for a momentary blaze but to ignite an unquenchable flame. Revival was never meant to be an exception; it was designed to be the norm. It is the breath of God filling us over and over, keeping us alive and flourishing in His presence. The question is not whether revival is available, but whether we are willing to embrace it.

The Breath Of Revival

Breathing is the simplest yet most essential rhythm of life. We inhale and exhale thousands of times a day, often without realizing it. Yet, the moment we stop breathing, life begins to slip away. Revival is much like this natural rhythm. Revival is the spiritual breath that sustains us. When God breathed life into Adam, it was not a one-time act, but the establishment of a pattern: life is sustained by the breath of God. Without it, our spirits begin to wither and fade away.

Every time we exhale, we expire. Without a fresh inhalation, life falters. Similarly, without continuous revival, fresh infillings of the Holy Spirit, our faith becomes stale, lifeless, and routine. Revival is the breath of God, drawing us back to life, not once but again and again. It's His invitation to live in the fullness of His presence. As Paul reminded Timothy, we must fan into flame the gift of God within us (2 Timothy 1:6). Revival is God's response to our surrender, His breath renewing our strength and restoring our purpose.

Revival always begins with an invitation. God is constantly calling His people to come closer, to go deeper, to live fully alive in Him. He never forces us. He will not drag us into His presence or demand our surrender. Instead, He patiently invites us, waiting for us to choose Him above all else. Revival is a banquet prepared, but the decision to sit at the table is ours.

Consider Jesus' parable of the wedding feast (Matthew 22). The invitations were sent far and wide, yet many refused to come. Some were too busy, others indifferent. Revival is no different. The invitation goes out to everyone, but not all will respond. Some will say, "Not now, Lord. I'm too overwhelmed, too distracted, too uncertain." Yet the invitation remains, waiting for the hungry, the thirsty, the desperate to step in.

God is looking for hearts that are willing. The question is not whether He is ready to move, but whether we are ready to receive. Revival is for those who want it more than anything else. It's for those who are tired of routine, weary of lifeless faith, and longing for a touch of heaven. Revival begins when we drop our conditions and excuses, surrendering fully to God's invitation.

The Love Language Of Repentance

Repentance is not a heavy burden; it is the love language of revival. It is how we draw near to God, how we keep our hearts tender and aligned with His. Acts 3:19 tells us, *"Repent, and turn to God, so that your sins may be wiped out, that times of refreshing may come from the Lord."* That phrase 'times of refreshing' is powerful. In Greek, the word *anapsyxis* translates directly to revival. Repentance is the doorway to refreshing, the pathway to life.

Just as no human relationship can thrive without forgiveness and reconciliation, our relationship with God requires repentance to remain vibrant. It's not about guilt or shame; it's about love. When we say, "Lord, I'm sorry," we're opening the door for His presence to flood our lives. A heart that repents is a heart that welcomes revival.

Without repentance, revival cannot be sustained. It is the foundation upon which God's glory rests. Holiness is not a list of rules but a posture of the heart, a willingness to align our lives with God's character. When we live in awe and repentance, we create a space where God's presence can dwell continuously. Revival flourishes in the soil of humility.

The High Places Must Fall

In ancient Israel, 'high places' were sites of idolatry, places where people worshipped other gods. Today, our high places may look different, but they are no less destructive. A high place is anything we elevate above God—our ambitions, comforts, or distractions. High places are the towers we build to reach heaven on our terms, but they fall short of true holiness.

Revival requires that we tear down these high places. Colossians 3:1-3 urges us, *"Set your hearts on things above, where Christ is, seated at the right hand of God. Set your minds on things above, not on earthly things.*" True revival demands that we forsake our high places and seek the heavenly places where Jesus reigns.

The call to revival is a call to total surrender. It's an invitation to dethrone anything that competes with God's rightful place in our lives. High places may seem harmless, even beneficial, but they keep us from experiencing the fullness of God's presence. Revival begins when we exchange our high places for His heavenly places.

Hunger That Touches Heaven

Revival is born out of hunger, an intense, unrelenting desire for God that refuses to settle for anything less than His presence. In the eighth chapter of Luke, we find a vivid example of this hunger in the story of a woman who made a demand on heaven with her desperate faith. Her encounter with Jesus is a powerful testament to the kind of hunger that draws the power of God into our lives.

Everywhere Jesus went, people gathered in droves, eager to hear His words and witness His miracles. The crowd was noisy, chaotic, and overwhelming, yet within it was a woman whose story sets her apart. For twelve long years, she had suffered from a condition that caused her to bleed continually, a physical ailment that was not only debilitating but also marked her as ceremonially unclean in her community. According to Jewish law, her condition rendered her an outcast, unable to participate in worship or even have normal relationships with others. She had spent everything she had on physicians, yet her condition had only worsened. She was at the end of herself, broken, isolated, and without hope in the natural.

But then she heard about Jesus. Word had spread that He was a healer, a man of miracles. Something ignited within her, a glimmer of hope and an unrelenting hunger for the healing and restoration she so desperately needed. She determined in her heart that she had to reach Him.

The woman made her way to where Jesus was, but the crowd was dense, and the odds were against her. She had no appointment with Him, no guarantee that He would even see her, let alone stop to help her. But her hunger fueled her faith, and her faith propelled her forward. She thought to herself, *"If I can only touch the hem of His garment, I will be made whole"* (Luke 8:44). She didn't need an audience with Jesus; she didn't even need Him to speak to her. She believed that His very presence was enough to heal her.

As Jesus walked, the woman pushed through the crowd, navigating the throngs of people who were likely oblivious to her struggle. Finally, with one last desperate reach, her fingers brushed the edge of His robe. In that moment, something extraordinary happened. Scripture says that immediately, her bleeding stopped, and she knew she was healed.

But the story doesn't end there. Jesus, feeling the touch, stopped and asked, "Who touched Me?" His disciples were incredulous. With the crowd pressing in on every side, they couldn't understand why Jesus would single out one touch. But Jesus knew this touch was different. *"Somebody touched Me,"* He said, *"for I perceived power going out from Me"* (Luke 8:46, NKJV).

Trembling, the woman came forward and fell at His feet. In front of everyone, she confessed why she had touched Him and how she had been instantly healed. Jesus, with compassion and affirmation, said to her, *"Daughter, your faith has made you well. Go in peace"* (Luke 8:48). In that moment, her faith, driven by her hunger, not only unlocked physical healing but also restored her dignity and identity as a beloved daughter of God.

This story teaches us a profound lesson about revival: it comes to those who hunger for God with a desperation that breaks through barriers. The woman didn't wait for an invitation or ideal circumstances.

Her hunger moved her beyond fear, rejection, and physical limitations to reach Jesus. She didn't demand His attention with words or deeds; her faith did the speaking, and her hunger made a demand on heaven that Jesus could not ignore.

In the same way, revival begins when we refuse to let anything stand between us and God. It is birthed in hearts that long for Him more than anything else, hearts that reach out in faith, believing that just one touch of His presence can change everything. Like the woman in Luke 8, we must press through the distractions, doubts, and obstacles in our lives to reach Him.

Revival people are those who live with this kind of hunger every day. They wake up with an unrelenting desire to encounter God, to draw near to Him, and to see His power manifest in their lives and the world around them. Just as Jesus felt power go out from Him when the woman touched His garment, He responds to the hungry hearts that reach out to Him today. The question is, will we be among the crowd, content to be near Him without truly encountering Him, or will we be like the woman who dared to touch Him, drawing power from His presence and sparking revival in our hearts and communities? The choice is ours, and revival is waiting.

Hunger is the currency of heaven. It's the cry that moves God's heart and releases His power. Revival is not reserved for the most talented or the most knowledgeable; it's for the hungry. It's for those who long to touch heaven and be transformed by it.

Right now, we are standing on the edge of something extraordinary. The Holy Spirit is stirring, moving across the earth in ways we cannot fully comprehend. It's a wave of revival, a fresh wind ready to crash on the shores of our lives. The question is, will we ride the wave or be swept under it?

This is not a time for complacency. God is shaking the foundations of what we have built, making room for His sovereignty to take center stage. The signs are all around us—wonders in the heavens, transformations on the earth. Revival is at the door, and it's calling us to step in.

When revival touches a church, it awakens a giant, transforms a culture, and moves a nation. It's not confined to walls or limited by traditions. It flows from a people hungry for God to a world desperate for hope. Revival is God's answer to a broken, weary world.

To live in revival is to live fully alive. It's to wake up each day with a heart ablaze, a spirit ignited, and a soul overflowing with God's presence. Revival is not about striving harder or doing more; it's about surrendering deeper and seeking more of Him. It's about allowing the Holy Spirit to continually renew and refresh us, keeping our faith vibrant and our lives fruitful.

Revival calls us out of complacency and into purpose. It's a reminder that we were not saved to sit on the sidelines but to live as active participants in God's kingdom. When we live in revival, we become carriers of His presence, bringing light to dark places and hope to hurting people.

This is the resurrected life, a life awakened by God, sustained by His Spirit, and marked by His power. It's not just for Sunday mornings or special occasions; it's for every moment of every day. Revival is a lifestyle, a choice to live fully alive in Christ.

The Invitation Remains

Revival is an invitation extended to everyone, but it's not an obligation. God will not force us into His presence, but He lovingly calls us to come. The decision is ours. Will we lay down our excuses, tear down our high places, and press into His presence? Or will we let this divine moment pass us by?

The invitation is clear: *"Draw near to God, and He will draw near to you"* (James 4:8, NKJV). Revival is not about waiting for God to move; it's about responding to His call. It's about seeking Him with all our hearts, trusting that He will meet us there.

Revival is not an event; it's an encounter. It's not a moment; it's a movement. It's the breath of God filling His people, awakening His church, and transforming His world. And it's your choice to step into it.

Will You Step In?

The clouds are gathering, the rain is coming, and the river is rising. Revival is here, ready to flood our lives with God's presence. But it's still an invitation. God is waiting for us to say yes, to surrender our plans, seek His face, and live fully alive in Him.

Don't settle for less when the fullness of God is available. Don't linger in high places when heavenly places are calling. Revival is not a distant dream; it's a present reality for those who will step in. Let's be a revival people. Let's live again. Let's embrace the invitation and step into the life God has prepared for us. The choice is yours: will you step into revival?

1

The Fears People Have About Revival

To live as revival people means to live with a purpose rooted in the eternal. Revival empowers believers to actively participate in God's mission, bringing heaven to earth in practical, tangible ways. It calls for a shift in mindset, seeing every interaction, every job, and every relationship as an opportunity to reflect God's glory. Revival people walk into a room and shift the atmosphere, not because of their own abilities, but because the Holy Spirit resides within them. This mission reflects the heart of Pentecost. Pentecost was just the beginning, a charge to carry revival wherever the Spirit leads.

Jesus modeled this perfectly during His earthly ministry. He not only preached the kingdom of heaven, but demonstrated its reality. Every miracle He performed was an illustration of what happens when heaven touches earth. When He healed the sick, cast out demons, and fed the hungry, He was revealing what it looked like for heaven to touch earth. Revival people are called to do the same. They carry the fire of Pentecost, not as a relic of the past, but as an active, living reality that transforms lives and brings hope to a broken world. They feed the hungry, not just with bread but with the bread of life. They clothe the naked, not only with garments but with the righteousness of Christ.

The Holy Spirit is central to this mission. Before the New Testament was written, the apostles were empowered by the Holy Spirit to walk in boldness, wisdom, and supernatural power. Acts is a testament to what happens when the Spirit leads: lives are transformed, miracles abound, and the gospel spreads like wildfire. This same Spirit is available to us today, equipping and empowering us to live as carriers of God's presence. Revival people know that it is not by their might or power, but by the Spirit that mountains move, and lives are changed. They embrace the Spirit not just as a helper, but as the very breath that sustains their mission.

However, it is not enough to know Scripture; we must also know the Spirit. The Word of God is powerful, but without the Spirit's illumination, it remains incomplete in its application. Revival people are those who seek the fullness of God—both Word and Spirit—knowing that this dynamic partnership brings about supernatural revelation and transformation. They do not simply memorize Scripture; they live it, allowing the Spirit to reveal its depths and empower its application. They understand that without the Spirit, the Word becomes a set of instructions; with the Spirit, it becomes a living force that changes everything it touches.

To live in revival means to live in expectation. Revival people wake up each day with the anticipation that God will move, that His Spirit will lead, and that His kingdom will expand. They understand that every moment is an opportunity to reflect heaven on earth, to bring God's love, justice, and truth into every sphere of life. Revival people walk with an awareness of divine appointments, seeing every encounter as an opportunity for God to move. They are walking in revival, knowing that the same Spirit who raised Christ from the dead lives in them and empowers them to live as conduits of heaven.

Revival people do not claim to have it all together, but they are committed to the journey of becoming more like Christ every day. They prioritize prayer, not as a duty but as a lifeline to the Father. They worship, not as a routine but as an overflow of their love for God. They repent quickly, knowing that revival cannot coexist with compromise or sin. They are not content with yesterday's manna; they seek fresh bread from heaven daily, believing that God's mercies are new every morning.

Living as revival people means embracing the discomfort of change. Revival disrupts routines and challenges the status quo. It requires a willingness to let go of old mindsets and traditions that hinder the move of God. Revival people are not afraid to stretch spiritually, to be poured into new wineskins that can contain the new wine God is pouring out. They understand that revival is not about their comfort but about His kingdom.

Revival is an invitation to encounter God's presence in a way that changes everything. Yet, with this opportunity comes fear. Revival after all is supernatural. Revival disrupts the status quo, challenges our comfort zones, and demands surrender. These fears, if left unchecked, can hold us back from experiencing the fullness of God's move. Below, we explore seven common fears people have about revival and how God's truth answers each one.

What If It's Weird?

Revival often looks unusual to those experiencing it for the first time. It pushes the boundaries of what we consider normal or comfortable. This fear stems from a desire for predictability and a reluctance to embrace what we don't fully understand. But consider this: who defines what is 'weird'? What may seem strange to us could be holy to God.

At Pentecost, the outpouring of the Holy Spirit came with tongues of fire and the sound of a rushing wind. To onlookers, it appeared chaotic, even leading some to accuse the disciples of being drunk. Yet, this 'weird' moment was the birth of the church, a holy event that ignited a global movement.

The discomfort we feel in these moments often reveals our resistance to relinquishing control. Revival requires us to trust God's ways over our preferences. The Apostle Paul reminds us, *"The foolishness of God is wiser than human wisdom, and the weakness of God is stronger than human strength."* (1 Corinthians 1:25). What we might call 'weird' could be God's way of working beyond our understanding.

True revival happens when we surrender to God's Spirit, even when it doesn't make sense to us. It calls us to trust that He knows what He is doing and to embrace the mystery of His presence. Instead of fearing the unfamiliar, we are invited to lean into it, knowing that God's ways are always perfect.

What If His Presence Messes With Our Nice Atmosphere?

For some, the fear of revival lies in its ability to disrupt the atmosphere they've carefully created. Churches often create environments designed for comfort, predictability, and community, but God's presence doesn't fit neatly into these spaces. His presence is holy, overwhelming, and all-consuming.

When revival comes, it exposes the idols we've created, even in the church. Have we built our gatherings around entertainment, personal preferences, or social connections? Revival disrupts these lesser pursuits, calling us back to the true purpose of the church: to glorify God and make His name known.

Paul's words in Ephesians 5:18 challenge us, *"Do not get drunk on wine, which leads to debauchery. Instead, be filled with the Spirit."* Many people drink deeply from the cup of comfort and culture but hesitate to drink from the well of the Holy Spirit. Revival flips this dynamic, calling us to prioritize His presence above all else.

When God's presence fills a room, it cannot be ignored. It challenges our indifference, awakens our spirits, and redirects our focus. This disruption is not something to fear but something to celebrate. It is evidence that God is moving and that His glory is taking center stage.

What If Our Denominational Comfort Zones, Traditional Doctrines, And Religious Systems Will Not Hold Or Cope When Revival Comes?

Revival often confronts the boundaries we've built around our faith. Denominations, doctrines, and traditions provide structure, but they can also become barriers when they limit our openness to God's movement. This fear stems from a desire to maintain control and a reluctance to let go of what feels familiar.

The Pharisees struggled with this during Jesus' ministry. They clung to their traditions so tightly that they missed the Messiah standing before them. Revival requires us to hold our theology with humility, recognizing that God is bigger than our systems.

Paul's instruction in 2 Corinthians 10:5 is clear: *"We demolish arguments and every pretension that sets itself up against the knowledge of God, and we take captive every thought to make it obedient to Christ."* Revival challenges us to tear down anything that exalts itself above God, even our religious constructs.

When revival comes, it may not fit within the frameworks we've established. It may challenge our doctrines or stretch our traditions. But rather than resisting it, we are called to trust that God is in control. He is not limited by our systems, and His plans are always perfect.

What If It Takes Over Everything And Our Other Things Won't Have Any Room Left?

Revival has a way of consuming everything in its path. It demands our time, attention, and resources. This can be intimidating for those who fear losing their routines or having to re-prioritize their lives. But the truth is, revival isn't something that competes with our plans—it re-orders them according to God's purposes.

Jesus said, *"Seek first his kingdom and his righteousness, and all these things will be given to you as well"* (Matthew 6:33). Revival calls us to put God first, trusting that everything else will fall into place. This shift in priorities may feel overwhelming, but it is also freeing. When God takes center stage, everything else finds its rightful place.

The fear of revival taking over stems from a misunderstanding of its purpose. Revival doesn't eliminate what is good in our lives; it refines it. It calls us to let go of what is temporary and embrace what is eternal. In doing so, we discover a deeper sense of purpose and fulfillment.

Revival is not a burden; it is a gift. It invites us to live fully for God, aligning our lives with His will. While it may require sacrifice, it also brings blessings beyond what we could imagine. The question is, are we willing to let God take over and trust Him with the results?

What If It Gets More Personal?

Revival is deeply personal. It isn't just about what God is doing in a church or community; it's about what He's doing in individual hearts. This intimacy can be intimidating for those who fear being exposed or called to change.

God's presence has a way of revealing what is hidden. It exposes sin, confronts pride, and challenges complacency. But this exposure is not meant to shame us; it is meant to heal us. When Isaiah encountered

God's holiness, he cried out, *"Woe to me! I am ruined!"* (Isaiah 6:5). Yet, God's response was not condemnation but cleansing.

Revival calls us to vulnerability. It invites us to lay our hearts bare before God, trusting that He will meet us with grace and mercy. It is through this process of surrender that we experience true transformation.

The fear of revival becoming personal often stems from a reluctance to let go of control. We worry about what God might ask of us or what He might reveal. But when we trust Him, we discover that His plans for us are always good. Revival is not about exposing our weaknesses; it is about revealing His strength in us.

What If I'm An Introvert And Cannot Be Moved?

Revival is for everyone, not just the extroverted or outspoken. The Holy Spirit moves in ways that transcend personality types. Whether you are an introvert or extrovert, God's presence is capable of transforming your life.

Consider the example of Moses. By his own admission, he was not an eloquent speaker, yet God used him to lead an entire nation out of slavery. Revival doesn't require charisma or confidence; it requires a willing heart. The fire of God ignites anyone who is open to Him, regardless of their personality.

When a piece of bacon hits a hot pan, it sizzles and curls, not because of the pig's temperament but because of the fire. Similarly, when we encounter the Holy Spirit, we are moved, not by our own abilities but by His power. Revival is not about how we feel, it's about what God is doing.

Introverts may experience revival differently than extroverts, but the impact is the same. It is not about external expressions but internal transformation. Revival meets us where we are and draws us closer to God, no matter our personality.

What If The World And The Community Resist Or Persecute Me For Moving In Revival?

Resistance is a natural part of revival. Whenever God moves, the enemy pushes back. This opposition can come from the world, the community, or even within the church. The fear of resistance often holds people back, but it is also a sign that we are on the right track.

Jesus warned His disciples, *"If the world hates you, keep in mind that it hated me first"* (John 15:18). Resistance is not a sign of failure; it is evidence that God's kingdom is advancing. Every great move of God has faced opposition because it threatens the enemy's strongholds.

Resistance can feel discouraging, but it is also an opportunity to grow in faith. It strengthens our dependence on God and refines our trust in His plans. Consider David facing Goliath, or the Israelites marching around Jericho. In each case, what appeared to be resistance was actually the pathway to victory.

Revival calls us to stand firm in the face of opposition, knowing that God is with us. It reminds us that we are not fighting for victory but from victory. As Paul wrote, *"If God is for us, who can be against us?"* (Romans 8:31). The fear of resistance is real, but it is no match for the power of God.

You Decide If You Want God's Fire

Revival, transformation, and spiritual power all hinge on a profound truth: whether the fire on your altar is burning or not is totally up to you. God provides the fire, but He entrusts its care to us. This truth is beautifully illustrated in Jesus' parable of the ten virgins (Matthew 25:1-13). Ten young women awaited the bridegroom, but only five brought oil for their lamps. The others. unprepared and lacking the means to sustain their flames, were shut out when the bridegroom arrived. This parable is a sobering reminder that preparation and stewardship are essential for those who wish to experience the fullness of God.

Five virgins carried oil, ensuring their lamps would burn brightly, while the other five foolishly assumed they could ride on the coattails of the moment without putting in the effort. The oil represents the fire of God in our lives—the anointing, passion, and presence of the Holy Spirit. Without it, we are left in darkness. This story echoes a central truth: sustaining the fire is our responsibility. God lights the flame, but we must fan it into a blaze.

Keeping The Fire Burning

The Bible gives clear instructions about maintaining God's fire. In Leviticus 6:13, God commanded the priests, *"The fire shall ever be burning upon the altar; it shall never go out."* This wasn't a suggestion, it was a divine mandate. The fire symbolized God's presence, and its constant burning demonstrated a life continually devoted to Him. Today, the principle remains the same: the fire on the altar of our hearts must be nurtured. It's not enough to experience God's presence once; we must cultivate a lifestyle that keeps His fire alive within us.

Paul echoes this call in 2 Timothy 1:6, reminding Timothy to *"fan into flame the gift of God."* This isn't passive; it's active. It requires intentionality, prayer, worship, and surrender. Revival isn't sustained by one emotional moment; it's sustained by daily choices to seek God and prioritize His presence. Without these choices, the fire dwindles.

The reality is stark: no power, no fire, no transformation will happen without the Holy Spirit's presence within us leading us deeper into God's presence. The Christian life without fire is nothing more than religion, routine and powerless. Revival is impossible without sacrifice, commitment, and accountability.

The most dangerous place for a Christian is not in persecution but in a world that demands no sacrifice, no commitment, and no accountability. In such an environment, the fire of God has nothing to hold onto. A life focused on comfort, pleasure, and convenience slowly withdraws the oxygen needed for spiritual vitality. Without passionate prayer, vibrant worship, and meaningful fellowship, the fire of God fades, leaving behind a form of godliness without power (2 Timothy 3:5).

Jesus warned of the lukewarm church in Revelation 3:16, saying He would spit them out of His mouth. Lukewarmness is dangerous because it lulls us into complacency. It allows the wood of faith to become wet, making it nearly impossible for the fire of God to burn. This is the devil's strategy: to replace fiery devotion with comfort and apathy.

The worship of other gods

One reason the fire goes out is that we place other things on the altar of our lives. Humanity's altars are never empty; something is always being worshipped. When God's fire doesn't burn, it's often because we've replaced Him with idols—comfort, success, reputation, or personal gratification. These false gods cannot sustain us, and they rob us of the intimacy we were designed to have with God.

The Bible is clear: *"You shall have no other gods before me"* (Exodus 20:3). God's fire cannot coexist with divided worship. When we prioritize ourselves, whether it be our convenience, ego, or pleasure over Him, we find it impossible to do what He asks. The most basic acts of obedience become burdensome when our hearts are not aligned with His.

Consider the story of Elijah on Mount Carmel (1 Kings 18). The prophets of Baal cried out to their god, cutting themselves and performing elaborate rituals, but no fire fell. Meanwhile, Elijah rebuilt the altar of the Lord, prayed a simple prayer, and God's fire consumed the offering, the wood, and even the water surrounding it. The difference was clear: the fire of God only falls where He alone is worshipped.

The cost of fire

Worship without sacrifice is unbiblical. Carrying God's fire comes at a cost. Romans 12:1 calls us to present our bodies as living sacrifices, holy and acceptable to God. Sacrifice is not easy, but it is essential. Fire consumes everything it touches, refining and purifying until only what is of God remains. For some, the fear of this refinement keeps them from fully surrendering.

The five foolish virgins weren't willing to pay the price of preparation. They wanted the reward without the sacrifice. But fire cannot burn without fuel and oxygen. In the same way, God's presence requires us to continually offer Him the fuel of our worship, obedience, and faith. Without these, the flame flickers and dies.

Jesus said, *"For everyone who asks receives"* (Matthew 7:8). If we want His fire, we must ask for it and prepare to steward it. Revival starts with a simple yes to God, a willingness to let His Spirit lead and transform us.

The church on fire

The early church in Acts provides a powerful example of what happens when believers embrace the fire of God. When the Holy Spirit fell on the disciples in the Upper Room, they were instantly transformed. These ordinary men and women became bold witnesses, filled with passion and power. The fire on their altar spread, igniting the world around them.

In Acts 2, Peter, once timid and prone to fear, stood before a crowd and preached with authority. Three thousand people were saved that day. The fire of God turned a hesitant fisherman into a bold leader. This transformation came directly from the Holy Spirit.

The early church wasn't perfect, but they were ablaze. They prayed fervently, worshipped passionately, and shared everything they had. Their fire wasn't fueled by programs or performances; it was fueled by the Holy Spirit. This fire sustained them through persecution, trials, and growth.

What about today? Many churches have traded fire for formality, boldness for business as usual. The same Holy Spirit who empowered the early church is available to us, but we must be willing to receive Him.

Fanning the flame

Keeping the fire burning is an active, daily process. It requires us to prioritize God's presence over everything else. Prayer, worship, fellowship, and obedience are the fuel and oxygen that keep the flame alive. Without them, the fire fades, and we risk falling into complacency.

Paul's words to Timothy are a challenge for us today: *"Fan into flame the gift of God"* (2 Timothy 1:6). This isn't something we can delegate to others, it's our responsibility. Revival starts in our hearts, and whether the fire burns or not depends on our willingness to nurture it.

This doesn't mean striving in our own strength. The Holy Spirit is the source of the fire, and He empowers us to steward it. But we must be intentional. We must choose to seek God, even when it's inconvenient. We must prioritize His presence, even when the world pulls us in other directions.

What will you decide?

Revival is an invitation, but it's also a decision. God provides the fire, but we must decide whether we'll fan it into a blaze or let it flicker out. Like the ten virgins, we must choose whether we'll prepare or be caught empty-handed. The choice is ours.

Are you willing to surrender your comfort, convenience, and idols for the fire of God? Are you ready to present yourself as a living sacrifice, allowing Him to refine and transform you? The fire on your altar depends on your yes to Him.

Without the fire of God, all we have is religion, rituals without power, and form without substance. But with His fire, we become fully alive, ignited by His Spirit and empowered to bring His kingdom to earth. Whether the fire burns brightly or fades away is up to you.

As Jesus said, *"For anyone who asks receives"* (Matthew 7:8). Will you ask Him for His fire today? Will you prepare your heart to steward His presence?

The choice is yours, and the time is now. Let the fire burn.

2

The Pre-Revival Battle

God woke me with these words:
"Wake up! Wake from sleep... WAR IS HERE!"

The resistance we're encountering should be good news to us! It is evidence we've hit a wall between where we've come from and where we're going. We look at resistance as something to be rebuked or avoided, but instead it should be something we celebrate and embrace as evidence we are breaking new ground and moving forward. The enemy uses resistance to stop people, but God uses resistance to test obedience, stretch faith and release promises. Make no mistake... the enemy is not afraid of us... He's afraid of what we can do when we remain pure and obey God! He knows that we are the gatekeepers of our own breakthrough. He understands in revival we become the outlet of heaven on earth, and we have the power to live in God's overflow. So, he brings resistance!

Goliath was not David's resistance... he was David's breakthrough!
Jericho was not the Israelites resistance... it was their breakthrough!
The cross was not Jesus' resistance... it was His breakthrough!
Your current frustrations are not your resistance... they are the things standing in the way of your breakthrough!

Revival doesn't come quietly. It comes with preparation, conflict, and purification. It comes with determination and faith. Before the fullness of God's presence falls, there is a necessary season of upheaval, a battle that separates the faithful from the complacent, the devoted from the distracted, and the lovers from the adulterers. This is the pre-revival battle, where lines are drawn, hearts are tested, and the church is prepared to carry the weight of God's glory.

This battle is not physical but spiritual. It is a fight for holiness, consecration, and alignment with God's kingdom. It's a war against apathy, compromise, and the schemes of the enemy. *Resist the devil, and he will flee from you.* (James 4:7) Every great move of God has been preceded by a season of battle, and this is no exception. The revival we have prayed for is coming, but before it arrives, God must cleanse and refine His house. As uncomfortable and troubling as that may sound it should not be feared. God is doing something so His people can be in revival.

Putting on the Armor of God

Paul's words in Ephesians 6:11-18 are more urgent now than ever: *"Put on the full armor of God, so that you can take your stand against the devil's schemes. For our struggle is not against flesh and blood, but against the rulers, against the authorities, against the powers of this dark world and against the spiritual forces of evil in the heavenly realms."*

The armor of God is essential. Without it, we are vulnerable to the enemy's attacks. Paul describes six critical pieces of armor, each representing a vital aspect of our spiritual defense:

1. The Belt of Truth

"Stand firm then, with the belt of truth buckled around your waist." (Ephesians 6:14)

The belt of truth is foundational. In Roman armor, the belt held the rest of the armor together, providing stability and readiness for battle. Spiritually, truth serves the same purpose: it anchors us. Without truth, every other piece of armor is compromised. Truth is not relative; it is absolute and rooted in the character and Word of God.

The enemy's primary tactic is deception. Jesus called Satan *"the father of lies"* (John 8:44). Lies lead to confusion, doubt, and spiritual weakness. But truth sets us free (John 8:32) and strengthens us to discern and resist the devil's schemes. Truth is not merely intellectual knowledge, but it is lived out in integrity and faithfulness. It holds everything together, ensuring our actions align with God's will.

To wear the belt of truth, immerse yourself in God's Word. Allow His truth to correct, guide, and uphold you. Walk in honesty and transparency, rejecting the compromises of falsehood. A life rooted in truth creates a solid foundation for standing firm.

2. The Breastplate of Righteousness
"With the breastplate of righteousness in place." (Ephesians 6:14)

The breastplate protects the heart and vital organs. In battle, it shields the soldier from fatal blows. Spiritually, the breastplate of righteousness guards our hearts from sin, guilt, and shame. Righteousness is not something we earn, but rather a gift from Christ, who became sin for us so that we might become the righteousness of God (2 Corinthians 5:21).

The heart is the center of our emotions, will, and desires. Proverbs 4:23 warns, *"Above all else, guard your heart, for everything you do flows from it."* The enemy seeks to corrupt our hearts with sin, self-righteousness, arrogance, pride or feelings of unworthiness. The breastplate protects us by reminding us that our righteousness comes from Christ, not our works.

Live in the righteousness provided by Jesus. Stay humble. Confess sin quickly and allow the Holy Spirit to transform your heart. Let your decisions, words, and actions reflect the righteousness of God. When accusations or temptations arise, stand firm, knowing your righteousness is secure in Christ.

3. The Gospel of Peace
"And with your feet fitted with the readiness that comes from the gospel of peace." (Ephesians 6:15)

Shoes may seem like an afterthought in armor, but for a soldier, they are essential. Roman soldiers wore sturdy, spiked sandals that provided stability and mobility, even on rough terrain. Spiritually, the gospel of peace equips us to stand firm and advance, no matter the circumstances. It is the assurance of our reconciliation with God and our role as messengers of His peace.

The gospel of peace empowers us to face life's chaos with confidence. Jesus said, *"Peace I leave with you; my peace I give you"* (John 14:27). This peace is not the absence of conflict but the presence of God's assurance in the storm. It steadies us in trials and propels us to share the gospel with a world in need.

Anchor your life in the peace of Christ. Trust His promises, even when circumstances seem overwhelming. Be ready to share the good news with others, walking boldly in your calling as an ambassador of Christ (2 Corinthians 5:20). Peace is both your defense and your mission.

4. The Shield of Faith
"Take up the shield of faith, with which you can extinguish all the flaming arrows of the evil one." (Ephesians 6:16)

The Roman shield was large enough to cover the entire body, providing protection against arrows and other attacks. Spiritually, the shield of faith defends us against the enemy's fiery darts; doubt, fear, temptation, and discouragement. Faith is our reliance on God's promises and character, even when we can't see the outcome.

The enemy's attacks are relentless. He sows seeds of doubt: *"Did God really say?"* (Genesis 3:1). He stokes fear, whispers lies and tempts us to abandon our trust in God. Faith shields us, extinguishing these flaming arrows and keeping us grounded in truth.

Faith comes by hearing the Word of God (Romans 10:17). Strengthen your faith through Scripture, prayer, and worship. Trust in God's faithfulness, even when circumstances test you. Lift the shield of faith daily, choosing to believe God's promises over the enemy's lies.

5. The Helmet of Salvation
"Take the helmet of salvation." (Ephesians 6:17)

The helmet protects the head, the seat of our mind and thoughts. Spiritually, the helmet of salvation guards our minds against doubt, fear, and confusion. Salvation is the assurance of our eternal security in Christ, but it also brings present deliverance from sin and its consequences.

The mind is a major battleground. The enemy seeks to infiltrate our thoughts, planting lies, doubts, and anxieties. The helmet of salvation reminds us of who we are in Christ: redeemed, loved, and secure. It protects us from the enemy's attempts to undermine our identity and destiny.

Renew your mind daily through the Word of God (Romans 12:2). Meditate on your salvation, what Christ has done for you and the hope you have in Him. Reject thoughts that contradict God's truth, taking every thought captive to make it obedient to Christ (2 Corinthians 10:5).

6. The Sword of the Spirit
"Take... the sword of the Spirit, which is the word of God." (Ephesians 6:17)

The sword is the only offensive weapon in the armor of God. It represents the Word of God, which is alive and active, sharper than any double-edged sword (Hebrews 4:12). The sword is both defensive and offensive, cutting through the lies of the enemy and advancing God's kingdom.

Jesus demonstrated the power of the Word when He was tempted in the wilderness. Each time Satan attacked, Jesus responded with Scripture: *"It is written"* (Matthew 4:1-11). The Word is our ultimate authority and weapon against the enemy's deception. It equips us to stand firm and push back the forces of darkness.

Study and memorize Scripture, allowing it to saturate your heart and mind. Use it in prayer, proclaiming God's promises over your life and circumstances. When the enemy attacks, respond with the truth of God's Word, declaring, *"It is written."*

To enter this battle unarmed is to invite defeat. Each piece of armor represents an intentional act of preparation, a declaration that we are ready to stand firm in the face of opposition.

Satan Has Been Recruiting In And Out Of The Church
He may have strongholds in the world, but he should not have any in the church. The enemy has been busy sowing seeds of deception, division, accusation, suspicion, infighting and distraction, not just in the

world but within the church itself. Stirring up strife, jealousy and disunity among leaders. We see the rise of the finger- pointing obsession within the body itself. This is not acceptable to God.

Jesus warned in Matthew 7:15, *"Watch out for false prophets. They come to you in sheep's clothing, but inwardly they are ferocious wolves."* Satan's recruitment is subtle, appealing to pride, ambition, and self-interest.

This is a battle that must happen to purify God's house. Idolatry, sin, impurity and filth have kept the church from her revival destiny for too long. Many churches have unknowingly allowed the enemy to infiltrate their ranks, prioritizing programs over prayer, popularity over purity, entitlement over service, and performance over presence. With demonic guidance, many respected men and woman have fallen by raising themselves up to be worshiped, admired, and have become ministry idols in God's house. This is not acceptable to God.

This battle for holiness will change that! God is sorting this out. *"For the time is come that judgment must begin at the house of God: and if it first begins with us, what shall the end be of them that obey not the gospel of God?"* (1 Peter 4:17, NKJV)

This will be a battle for consecration, holiness and faith. It will clearly shine on those who live to follow Jesus and those who don't! This pre-revival battle will expose compromises, revealing who truly serves God and who has aligned with the enemy's agenda.

Satan has done this before. This is not a new tactic. Consider Judas Iscariot, one of Jesus' own disciples. Outwardly, he appeared devoted, but inwardly, he harbored pride, greed and betrayal. John 12:6 tells us that Judas stole from the money bag, even as he walked with Jesus. Helped himself when Jesus asked him to serve others. When the moment came, he sold the Savior for thirty pieces of silver. Judas is a sobering reminder that proximity to Jesus is not the same as devotion to Him.

The enemy's recruitment thrives in the shadows, where unaddressed sin and unchecked pride fester. This battle will shine a light on these dark corners, forcing every believer to stand in the light and choose whom they will serve.

The Coming Battle Will Draw A Line Between Kingdoms

In 1 Corinthians 11:19, Paul writes, *"No doubt there have to be differences among you to show which of you have God's approval."* This battle will bring clarity, separating the sheep from the goats, the devoted from the distracted, and the holy from the hypocritical.

Jesus demonstrated this separation in Matthew 16:23 when He rebuked Peter, saying, *"Get behind me, Satan! You are a stumbling block to me; you do not have in mind the concerns of God, but merely human concerns."* Peter's intentions may have seemed noble, but they were rooted in human reasoning, not divine revelation.

This battle will force every believer to examine their allegiance. Are we building God's kingdom or our own? Are we aligned with His Spirit or driven by our deepest fleshly desires? The line between kingdoms will be unmistakable, and every heart will be tested.

We have to pick our side

Jesus said: *"I came to set fire to the earth, and I wish it were already on fire!"* (Luke 12:49, CEV) There is a pre-revival movement that calls us to pick our side. REVIVAL FLAMES are attractive to the lover, but offensive to the adulterer. To the unprepared He is a consuming fire (Hebrews 12:29) that threatens their way of life, their pride and their religion, but to the prepared He is a refiner who loves to purify, restore and bless!

Revivals are two-way streets. Past moves of God have shown us that many come rushing in, and some also leave. Some become grafted deeper into what God is stirring in their heart, and others choose to remove themselves from the vine for a place with less commitment. This is what revival does. It requires people to decide which side they want to be on.

The days of lukewarm faith are over. Revelation 3:16 warns, *"So, because you are lukewarm—neither hot nor cold—I am about to spit you out of my mouth."* In this battle, neutrality is not an option. Every believer must choose a side, declaring their allegiance to God or the world.

Elijah posed the same challenge to Israel in 1 Kings 18:21: *"How long will you waver between two opinions? If the Lord is God, follow him; but if Baal is God, follow him."* The time for wavering is past. The pre-revival battle demands a decision.

Hiding is no longer possible. The enemy's schemes are coming to light, and God is calling His people to step out of the shadows. Those who try to remain neutral will find themselves swept away by the tide of spiritual conflict. This is not a time for passive faith; it is a time for bold declaration.

The Battle Is An Answer To Your Prayers

Many of us have prayed for revival, asking God to pour out His Spirit and transform the church. This battle is His answer. Before revival can come, there must be purification. Before the Holy Spirit can rest upon us, there must be repentance.

Malachi 3:2-3 describes this process: *"But who can endure the day of his coming? Who can stand when he appears? For he will be like a refiner's fire or a launderer's soap. He will sit as a refiner and purifier of silver."*

This refining is not punishment; it is preparation. It is God's way of readying His people to carry the weight of His glory.

The battle may be uncomfortable, but it is necessary. It is the pathway to the revival we have longed for. Let us not resist the refining fire but embrace it, trusting that God's plans are always for our good.

This Is Urgent! There Is No Time To Waste

Romans 13:11 declares, *"And do this, understanding the present time: The hour has already come for you to wake up from your slumber, because our salvation is nearer now than when we first believed."* The time for complacency is over. The battle is here, and we must act with urgency.

Too often, we delay obedience, waiting for a more convenient time. But the stakes are eternal, and the opportunity before us is fleeting. The pre-revival battle demands immediate action.

Let us heed the call to wake up, to shake off apathy and indifference. The hour is late, and the harvest is plentiful. Will we rise to the occasion, or will we be found sleeping when the bridegroom comes?

Start With A Well-Oiled Prayer Meeting

Revival begins with prayer—fervent, Spirit-led intercession that shakes the heavens. Pentecost came to a group of believers who were gathered in unity, praying and waiting on the Lord (Acts 2:1-4). It did not come to a carefully planned program or a meticulously executed service. It came to a prayer meeting.

The church today must rediscover the power of prayer. Whenever we have a passion for prayer rising in our churches, we also see greater moves of Holy Spirit in our services. You cannot have one without the other.

Too often, we prioritize activities over intimacy, programs over presence. But the revival we long for will not come through human effort. It will come through hearts surrendered in prayer.

Let us gather, not out of obligation but out of desperation. Let us cry out for God to move, not in our way but in His. A well-oiled prayer meeting is the foundation of every great move of God.

Jesus Is Coming Back For His Church

This battle is not an end in itself; it is preparation for the return of Christ. Revelation 22:17 proclaims, *"The Spirit and the bride say, 'Come!' And let the one who hears say, 'Come!'"* Jesus is coming back for a church that is holy, pure, and ablaze with His glory. Can I tell you something VERY important ... Jesus is NOT coming back for a church that is less POWERFUL than the one He left! The church He will come back for will look like the one He made and not the one we made.

The pre-revival battle is God's way of readying His bride. It is a call to wake up, clean house, and align ourselves with His kingdom. This is not a time for fear but for faith. The King is coming, and His reward is with Him (Revelation 22:12).

Are you ready for the battle? Are you prepared for His return? The time is now to put on the armor of God, take your stand, and fight for the kingdom. The pre-revival battle is here. So, wake up, church, and take your place in His army.

3

A Move Of Restoration

This is a word for somebody today: **God is moving in restoration.** What you thought was lost forever, what the enemy stole from you, and what was broken beyond repair. These are the very things God is about to redeem. This is not just a wave of revival, but a move of restoration. Revival brings new life, but restoration takes what was lost and brings it back, multiplied.

I heard God say: *"Nobody else is allowed to build with the bricks that I've given you!"* You have lost things unfairly and without God's consent. These losses—your joy, your opportunities, your relationships, even your dreams—were never meant to be stolen. God's word over you has not changed. What was illegitimately taken will be returned, and more.

"If the thief is caught, he must pay back seven times what he stole, even if he has to sell everything in his house to make it right." (Proverbs 6:31, NLT) This is the promise of restoration, and it is for you today.

Thieves Take What Is Not Theirs

Thieves are not creators. They have no right to what they take. Yet, they steal to satisfy their greed, to fill a void they cannot explain. Just as in the natural, thieves in the spiritual realm take what they cannot create: joy, peace, purpose, and relationships. The enemy is the ultimate thief, but he has no lasting power.

Jesus exposed this truth in John 10:10 (NKJV): *"The thief does not come except to steal, and to kill, and to destroy. I have come that they may have life, and that they may have it more abundantly."*

The devil's mission is clear: to steal what God has given you, to kill your hope, and to destroy your destiny. But he is a defeated foe. Jesus came to reverse every one of the enemy's schemes, restoring life and multiplying His blessings.

God's gifts to you are sacred. They are not random or disposable; they are purposeful, handpicked for your life. When the enemy steals, he is not just attacking you and he is defying God. But the Lord sees every theft and has promised justice. Isaiah 61:8 reads, *"For I, the Lord, love justice; I hate robbery and wrongdoing. In my faithfulness I will reward my people and give them their recompense."*

Your health, family, ministry, and joy are not up for grabs. These gifts were placed in your care by the One who owns all things. When the thief takes, God's justice demands restoration. And not just restoration but abundance. Seven-fold.

Seven-fold restoration is more than a number; it is a declaration of divine completion and perfection. It signifies that God will not only return what was stolen but will add to it until it overflows with His goodness. Expect the places of your greatest losses to become the places of your greatest breakthroughs.

Recognizing The Thief

Has the thief in your life been caught yet? Sometimes the enemy works subtly, stealing in ways we don't immediately recognize. Perhaps it's a relationship that quietly unraveled, a dream you slowly gave up on, or a peace that slipped away over time.

But as the Spirit moves in this season of restoration, He is shining a light into the shadows. Thieves cannot hide in the presence of God's glory. What has been hidden will be revealed, and what has been stolen will be repaid.

Think about Job. In a single day, he lost everything, his wealth, his children, his health. It seemed as though the thief had won. But Job remained faithful, and God restored to him twice what he had lost (Job 42:10). Restoration came not because Job demanded it but because God's justice demanded it.

In the same way, God sees your losses. He hears your cries. He is exposing the thief and preparing to restore what was taken.

Restoration begins when we bring our losses to God. Don't hold back or minimize your pain. Lay it all before Him; every broken dream, every stolen opportunity, every loss that left you wondering if you could ever recover.

Psalm 34:18 reminds us, *"The Lord is close to the brokenhearted and saves those who are crushed in spirit."* God's heart is moved by your pain. He is not indifferent to your losses. But restoration requires surrender. When we hold on to our bitterness or try to fix things in our own strength, we delay the process.

Take a moment to pray:
"Lord, I bring before You everything that has been lost, stolen, or broken in my life. I trust You to make it right. Restore what the enemy has taken and multiply it for Your glory."

Restoration Is Costly For The Thief

When God restores, it is not without cost to the enemy. Proverbs 6:31 (NLT) makes this clear: *"If the thief is caught, he must pay back seven times what he stole, even if he has to sell everything in his house to make it right."*

Every scheme of the enemy to rob you will backfire. The cost of stealing from God's children is severe, and the devil will pay. His resources are limited, but God's justice is unlimited. For every tear you've cried, every loss you've endured, and every setback you've faced, God is preparing a seven-fold restoration.

In Joel 2:25 (KJV), God promises, *"I will restore to you the years that the locust has eaten."* The locusts, representing devastation, may have stripped away your harvest, but they cannot destroy God's ability to restore. He doesn't just give back time; He redeems it, filling it with blessings that exceed what was lost.

All Thievery Comes From The Devil

The root of all theft is the devil himself. He is the original thief, seeking to destroy the goodness of God's creation. But his power is no match for the authority of Christ.

When Jesus died on the cross, He disarmed the powers and authorities of darkness, triumphing over them (Colossians 2:15). The victory was complete, leaving no room for the enemy to claim what does not belong to him. Restoration is not a possibility; it is a promise.

The enemy's tactics are crafty, but they are no match for the light of Christ. When we live in His light, the thief's schemes are exposed, and God's justice is enacted.

Prayers For Restoration

As we step into this season of restoration, let us pray with boldness:

Pray for those who stole from you!

Heavenly Father, we lift up to You those who have taken from us, knowingly or unknowingly, through their actions or as instruments of the enemy. We pray that You would soften their hearts and open their eyes to the truth. Let Your light shine into the darkness they are walking in, exposing their actions not to condemn but to draw them to repentance.

Lord, we ask that You grant them a moment of divine clarity, where they see the weight of their wrongdoing and are moved to seek forgiveness—not just from us but from You. Let them encounter Your mercy, the kind that transforms hearts and breaks chains. Pour out Your grace upon them, so they are not consumed by guilt or shame but are instead led into the freedom that comes through Jesus Christ.

Father, teach us to release the hurt, anger, and frustration we may feel toward those who have stolen from us. Help us to forgive them fully, not because they deserve it but because You have forgiven us. May our prayers for their repentance and restoration be a reflection of Your heart—a heart that always seeks redemption over destruction.

Pray for those restored

Gracious God, as You restore what the enemy has stolen and bring new life to the broken places, we thank You for Your faithfulness. You are the God who restores abundantly, who multiplies what was lost and turns mourning into dancing. We stand in awe of Your power to make all things new.

As we receive Your restoration, Lord, grant us the wisdom to handle it well. Teach us to be good stewards of the blessings You are pouring into our lives. Let us hold these gifts loosely, always remembering that they come from You and are meant to glorify Your name. Show us how to use what You've restored to bless others, build Your kingdom, and advance Your purposes on earth.

Father, guard our hearts against pride or complacency. Let us never forget the journey we've been through or the grace that carried us. May our lives be living testimonies of Your goodness and faithfulness, drawing oth-

ers to know You. As we walk in this season of restoration, let our gratitude overflow into acts of love, service, and worship.

Pray for yourself

Father, I come before You with an open and expectant heart. You see the broken places in my life, the losses I have endured, and the dreams that have been shattered. I lay them all before You, trusting in Your promise to restore what has been stolen and redeem what has been broken.

Lord, I invite You into every area of my life that needs healing. Pour out Your Spirit and bring renewal where there has been pain, hope where there has been despair, and joy where there has been mourning. Teach me to trust Your timing and Your ways, even when the restoration process feels slow or uncertain.

I declare today that I am ready to receive Your restoration. Let my heart be soft and open to Your work in me. Where there are old wounds or lingering bitterness, wash them away with Your love. Where fear or doubt has crept in, replace it with bold faith and unshakable trust in Your power.

Multiply Your blessings in my life, not just for my sake but for the sake of Your glory. Let the restoration I experience become a testimony to those around me of Your goodness and faithfulness. And Lord, as I step into this new season, help me to walk in gratitude, humility, and unwavering devotion to You. You are the God who makes all things new, and I trust You to do it in my life. Amen.

Job's Restoration

The story of Job stands as a timeless testament to God's power to restore, even in the face of unimaginable loss. Job was a man who walked blamelessly before God, yet he endured devastating trials. In a single day, his wealth was stripped away, his children were killed, and his health deteriorated as painful sores covered his body. Adding to his suffering, his friends accused him of hidden sin, and his wife urged him to curse God and die. Despite all this, Job remained steadfast in his faith, declaring,

"The Lord gave and the Lord has taken away; may the name of the Lord be praised" (Job 1:21).

God was fully aware of Job's suffering. It wasn't a random occurrence, nor was it unnoticed by the Creator.

Job's losses were the result of a spiritual challenge where Satan sought to prove that Job's faith was conditional. Yet, even in the depth of his pain, Job did not abandon his trust in God. This reminds us that nothing we endure escapes God's attention. He is deeply invested in our lives, watching over every detail with care and purpose. As Psalm 56:8 tells us, God collects every tear and records every sorrow. Job's story is a reminder that our pain matters to God, and restoration is always part of His plan.

The enemy's attacks are temporary and finite. Though Satan was permitted to test Job, he was bound by God's authority. *"Very well, then, he is in your hands; but you must spare his life"* (Job 2:12). This limitation shows that no matter how severe the trial, it cannot extend beyond what God allows. The enemy may steal, kill, and destroy, but his power is no match for God's sovereignty. For every loss the enemy orchestrates, God prepares a far greater restoration.

Job's restoration wasn't immediate, and it required enduring faith. Throughout his trials, Job cried out to God with raw honesty. He questioned, lamented, and expressed his confusion, but he never turned away from God. This perseverance became the foundation for his eventual breakthrough. Often, the path to restoration involves waiting and trusting God through the darkest valleys. Job's story teaches us that restoration is not a matter of 'if' but 'when'. God is always faithful to His promises, even when the timeline feels uncertain.

When God finally intervened, the restoration was overwhelming. Job 42:10 tells us that after Job prayed for his friends, God restored his fortunes and gave him twice as much as he had before. His wealth was multiplied, his family was renewed, and his health was restored. This was not merely a return to his former life but an abundance that exceeded his greatest expectations. Job's life demonstrates that God's restoration is never a one-to-one repayment, but rather a multiplication of blessing that reflects His generosity and justice.

More importantly, Job's restoration included spiritual renewal. At the end of his trials, Job declared, *"My ears had heard of you, but now my eyes have seen you"* (Job 42:5). Through his suffering, Job came to know God in a deeper and more intimate way. Restoration is not just about regaining what was lost; it's about gaining a greater understanding of God's character and experiencing His presence in a transformative way.

Job's story also highlights the importance of intercession. His restoration began when he prayed for his friends, the very ones who had accused him of wrongdoing. This act of humility and obedience unlocked the floodgates of God's blessing. It reminds us that restoration is often tied to forgiveness and a willingness to intercede for others, even those who have hurt us.

Job's journey shows that God's justice is certain. The thief may appear to succeed for a time, but he will always be caught and made to repay. Proverbs 6:31 (NLT) declares, *"If the thief is caught, he must pay back seven times what he stole, even if he has to sell everything in his house."* The losses you have experienced are not forgotten, and God's promise of restoration will not fail. The enemy's schemes will backfire, and you will see God's justice in action.

Job's story is an invitation to trust in God's restorative power. It reminds us that no loss is too great, no wound too deep, and no situation too broken for God to redeem. What the enemy meant for harm, God will turn for good. Trust Him to restore not just what was taken but to bring you into a season of abundance, spiritual renewal, and unshakable faith. God's restoration is always worth the wait.

Restoration Is A Move Of Revival

This move of restoration is inseparable from revival. As God revives His people, He restores what was lost, broken, or stolen. It is a twofold work, bringing new life and reclaiming what the enemy tried to take.

Isaiah 61:3 (NLT) declares, *"To all who mourn in Israel, he will give a crown of beauty for ashes, a joyous blessing instead of mourning, festive praise instead of despair."* God doesn't just replace our losses—He transforms them into something far greater.

This is a word for you today: The places of your greatest losses will become the places of your greatest breakthroughs. Restoration is not just about getting back what was taken; it is about stepping into the fullness of God's promises. Seven-fold. Multiplied. Perfected.

Let this season of restoration be a reminder that nothing is beyond God's redemption. Bring everything before Him, trust in His justice, and watch as He restores what you thought was gone forever. This is not the end. It is the beginning of a move of restoration that will leave you in awe of His goodness.

4

Demanding More

A true revival will demand more. It will not come from simply adding God to a part of your life, your schedule, or your church service. Revival is a total transformation. To grasp even a glimpse of God's holiness is to tremble at the reality of our humanity. Holiness is the foundation of revival, and without it, any move claiming to be from God is nothing more than a fleeting emotional experience.

God's revivals don't measure success by numbers, emotional responses, or even miracles. True revival is marked by repentance, a reverence for God's presence, and a rejection of sin. It draws people to run from sin with all their might and to pursue God with all their hearts. As James 4:8 (NKJV) says, *"Draw near to God, and He will draw near to you."* This is the essence of revival—to be wholly separated from the world and wholly dedicated to the presence of God.

The pursuit of holiness is non-negotiable. Hebrews 12:14 (NKJV) warns, *"Pursue peace with all people, and holiness, without which no one will see the Lord."* Holiness doesn't come by accident; it requires intentionality. We are called to cleanse ourselves from all defilement of flesh and spirit, as Paul exhorts in 2 Corinthians 7:1 (NKJV), *"perfecting holiness in the fear of God."* Yet, holiness is not something we can achieve on our own; it is a work of God in a yielded life.

John the Baptist foresaw this when he prophesied about Jesus, describing Him as One who comes with an axe in one hand and a winnowing fan in the other (Matthew 3:10-12). These tools represent God's refining work: the axe to cut away what is unfruitful and the fan to stoke the flames of revival. God's holiness is a consuming fire (Hebrews 12:29), burning away anything that doesn't align with His nature. Revival demands that we surrender everything to this refining fire, trusting that the transformation it brings will lead us closer to Him.

Revival will inevitably separate the things of God from the things of the world. It will draw a line in the sand and call us to make a choice. When God moves in power, there can be no middle ground. We cannot serve both God and the world (Matthew 6:24). The work of the Holy Spirit in revival isn't to create a feel-good moment but to glorify God and align our lives with His purposes (John 16:13-14).

This refining process may feel uncomfortable, but it is necessary. Jesus is returning for a church without spot or wrinkle, a holy bride prepared for her bridegroom. Revival is part of that preparation. It calls us to examine our lives, repent of sin, and recommit ourselves to God's purposes. Anything less is incomplete.

Holiness isn't just a requirement for revival; it's the very fuel that sustains it. As the saying goes, *"When you bring the wood, God will provide the fire."* Our role is to bring lives that are clean and surrendered, ready to burn brightly for His glory. In the upper room, the disciples waited in unity and prayer, positioning themselves to receive the Holy Spirit. When the fire fell, it wasn't just for them; it ignited a movement that would change the world. The same is true today.

Jesus said, *"Blessed are the pure in heart, for they will see God"* (Matthew 5:8). A pure heart isn't one without flaws but one fully committed to God, free from divided loyalties. Revival calls us to this kind of purity, to be a people set apart, ready to carry His presence to the world.

I believe God is saying, *"It doesn't matter what the world looks like right now. You are standing at the door of exceptional favor."* This is a season of convergence, where everything God has been preparing you for is coming together. It may not look like it on the surface. Joseph didn't look like a ruler while he was in prison, but God is always working behind the scenes. Just as Joseph was elevated to fulfill God's plan during a time of famine, so too is God preparing His people for a time of spiritual hunger.

Joseph's story is one of perseverance and preparation. His brothers tried to silence him, sell him, and destroy his destiny, but what they meant for evil, God used for good (Genesis 50:20). In the same way, many of God's chosen ones have been underestimated, sidelined, and blocked. Yet these are the very people God is raising up in this season. Revival flames are being ignited in the lives of the overlooked, the underestimated, and the faithful.

The door of exceptional favor is unlocked, and God is calling His people to step into their purpose. This is not the time to hesitate or doubt. Just as Pharaoh said, *"Go to Joseph; whatever he says to you, do"* (Genesis 41:55, NKJV), the world will turn to God's chosen ones in times of crisis. Revival isn't just about spiritual renewal; it's about positioning God's people to bring His solutions to a broken world.

This move of God will be marked by those who have surrendered everything. The men and women God is raising up are not those seeking fame or recognition but those who have been refined in the fire of surrender. They know what it means to lay everything down for the sake of the call.

Elijah's Story

The story of Elijah and the prophets of Baal on Mount Carmel is a profound example of God demanding more and showing His holiness through revival. During a time when the people of Israel wavered between worshiping God and following the false god Baal, Elijah stood as a lone prophet calling them back to full surrender. The nation was in spiritual drought, just as the land had experienced a physical drought for three years. This was no coincidence. God used the lack of rain to expose their lack of faithfulness and to prepare their hearts for a decisive moment of choosing whom they would serve.

Elijah's challenge to the people was direct and uncompromising. He asked, *"How long will you waver between two opinions? If the Lord is God, follow Him; but if Baal is God, follow him"* (1 Kings 18:21). The people said nothing in response, a silence that revealed their divided hearts. They wanted the benefits of worshiping God but were unwilling to give up their allegiance to Baal. This reflects the same tension many experience today, wanting revival without complete surrender, seeking God's blessings while holding onto worldly comforts.

On Mount Carmel, Elijah prepared for a demonstration of God's power that would demand a decision from the people. He proposed a test: both he and the prophets of Baal would prepare sacrifices, but neither would light the fire. Instead, they would call on their respective gods, and the one who answered with fire would be the true God. The prophets of Baal cried out all day, shouting, dancing, and even cutting themselves to try to provoke their god into action. But there was no response. Baal was silent because he was powerless, a false god incapable of meeting the demands of his worshippers.

Elijah's approach, in contrast, was marked by reverence and preparation. He repaired the altar of the Lord, which had been neglected and broken down. This act alone was a powerful symbol of restoration, a call to rebuild what had been forsaken. He used twelve stones to represent the twelve tribes of Israel, signifying their covenant relationship with God. Then, he drenched the altar with water, not once but three times, making it clear that no human effort could ignite the fire. This was a moment for God alone to act.

When Elijah prayed, his words were simple but profound. He didn't plead or perform; he simply asked God to reveal Himself so that the people would know He was the one true God and turn their hearts back to Him. *"Answer me, Lord, answer me, so these people will know that You, Lord, are God, and that You are turning their hearts back again"* (1 Kings 18:37). Instantly, the fire of the Lord fell, consuming not only the sacrifice but also the wood, the stones, the soil, and even the water in the trench. This was no ordinary fire; it was a consuming fire that left no doubt about God's power and holiness.

The people's response was immediate. They fell prostrate and cried out, *"The Lord—He is God! The Lord—He is God!"* (1 Kings 18:39). Revival broke out as they recognized their sin and returned to worshiping the true God. Elijah then commanded the people to seize the prophets of Baal, ensuring that the source of their idolatry was removed from the land. This wasn't just a moment of spiritual renewal; it was a decisive act of turning away from sin and reclaiming their identity as God's people.

This story is a powerful reminder that revival demands more than emotional enthusiasm or surface-level commitment. It requires a complete turning away from false gods and a wholehearted return to the Lord. Just as the fire consumed everything on the altar, God's revival will burn away anything in our lives that doesn't align with His holiness. Elijah's actions also teach us the importance of preparation—rebuilding the altar, offering what we have to God, and trusting Him to provide the fire.

The lesson here is clear: God demands complete surrender. We cannot waver between two opinions or try to serve both God and the world. Revival comes when we rebuild what has been broken, lay everything on the altar, and trust God to ignite His fire in our lives. Like the people of Israel, we are called to a moment of decision—to recognize that the Lord alone is God and to give Him our full allegiance. When we do, we can be confident that His consuming fire will not only purify us but also draw others to know and worship Him. This is the essence of revival: a move of restoration, purification, and transformation that demands everything but gives back infinitely more.

Step Into The Fire

To those who have been faithful, God is saying: *"Your time of testing has passed. You have waited, persevered, and remained faithful. Now, the door is open. Step through it with boldness."* The revival that is coming will require courage and faith. It will demand everything, but it will also release unimaginable blessings.

God is not looking for perfection; He is looking for hearts that are fully His. As we step into this season, let us remember that revival isn't just an event—it's a transformation that demands more of us than we've ever given before. But with that surrender comes the fullness of God's presence, the power of His Spirit, and the joy of seeing lives changed for His glory.

This is the season to press in, to demand more of ourselves, and to surrender fully to God's purposes. The revival flames are burning—let them consume everything that doesn't align with Him. Step into the fire, and watch as God uses you to bring His kingdom to earth.

5

Let Your Love Spark a Revival

Do you want to leave your mark on the world? In God, you can, and not just for a moment, but for eternity. What comes from your mouth, spoken in faith and filled with love for Jesus, has the potential to change lives, shift atmospheres, and even spark movements that transform nations.

Your love for God can spark a revival. Just think about the woman who reached out to touch the hem of Jesus' garment or Zacchaeus crying out to Jesus from a tree or blind Bartimaeus shouting from the beggar's place on the side of the road. Sometimes God touches us, but sometimes we get to touch God. There is biblical example for both. It is exciting to realize that some of the most incredible revivals were birthed when hunger in people reached the place where they abandoned all logic, etiquette and comforts to reach out with all their love and desperation to touch Him.

The Welsh Revival of 1904 began not with grand strategies or elaborate programs but with a single, trembling declaration from a young woman named Florrie Evans: *"I LOVE JESUS CHRIST – WITH ALL MY HEART!"* Her words were not rehearsed, and they weren't spoken for applause. They came from a place of raw surrender, born out of desperation and a deep yearning to be fully aligned with God.

Just a week before that declaration, Florrie sat with her pastor, Joseph Jenkins, overwhelmed by the state of her soul. She confessed, *"The matter of my soul is almost killing me. I cannot live like this. The world has a pervasive grip on me, and I am under its feet. I can't save myself. I am desperate. Help me."* Jenkins responded with a profound challenge: *"Can you say, 'MY LORD,' to Jesus Christ? Have you ever really surrendered EVERYTHING to Him?"*

Those words haunted her in the days that followed, stirring something deep within her spirit. God was asking for more—not just a part of her life but the entirety of her heart, soul, and will. That surrender came to fruition in a small church gathering, where Florrie's trembling voice cut through the silence: *"I LOVE JESUS CHRIST – WITH ALL MY HEART!"*

That single declaration acted as a match striking dry wood. W.T. Stead, a journalist who witnessed the revival, described the impact: *"The passion of that young girl acted like an electric shock upon the entire congregation. One after another rose and made their full surrender. Like wildfire, the news spread that revival had broken out. This whole thing is of God."*

Within two months of Florrie's declaration, over 70,000 people came to faith in Christ. Worship and repentance swept through Wales like a mighty wind, transforming lives, families, and entire communities. This wasn't a carefully orchestrated event; it was a divine outpouring, ignited by the surrendered cry of one heart.

Revival flowed wherever people opened their mouths to declare their love for Jesus, often through heartfelt songs. Singing became the lifeblood of the Welsh Revival. One observer remarked, *"The revival follows the track of the singing people. Wherever there is song, the Spirit moves."* These were not polished performances but spontaneous outpourings of devotion that filled the air with God's presence.

The simplicity of this movement reveals a powerful truth: revival doesn't require perfection; it requires surrender. Florrie's declaration wasn't born from fullness but from emptiness. She came to the end of herself, recognizing her inability to save or sustain her own soul, and in that moment of vulnerability, God's power was made perfect.

This is the essence of revival. It begins when we stop striving and start surrendering, when we stop clinging to control and cry out to God with everything we have. Revival is not about adding God to parts of our lives; it's about giving Him everything and allowing His Spirit to fill every corner of our hearts.

What comes from your mouth has the power to ignite something extraordinary. Think of the prophet Isaiah, who encountered God's holiness in a vision and cried out, *"Woe to me! I am ruined! For I am a man of unclean lips"* (Isaiah 6:5). In that moment of surrender, God purified Isaiah and commissioned him to carry His message. Similarly, when Florrie Evans cried out her love for Jesus, it wasn't just a personal act of devotion—it was a declaration that resonated with those around her, drawing them into the same surrender and devotion.

Revival doesn't start in comfort zones. It begins when people are willing to step out in boldness, even when their voices tremble. It begins when someone dares to say, *"I LOVE JESUS CHRIST – WITH ALL MY HEART,"* without fear of judgment or rejection. Florrie's words were electrifying because they came from a place of authenticity, and authenticity carries power. When others heard her declaration, they were compelled to respond, not because of her eloquence but because of the Spirit of God moving through her.

This principle is just as true today as it was in 1904. The cry of surrender from your heart—spoken or sung—has the potential to spark revival in your home, your church, your community, and beyond. God isn't looking for perfect voices or polished speeches. He's looking for hearts that are fully His, hearts that will cry out in love and devotion regardless of the circumstances.

Consider the story of King David bringing the ark of the covenant back to Jerusalem. As the ark entered the city, David danced before the Lord with all his might, wearing only a linen ephod (2 Samuel 6:14). His worship was unrestrained, and his love for God was on full display. When his wife Michal criticized him for his undignified behavior, David responded, *"I will celebrate before the Lord. I will become even more undignified than this"* (2 Samuel 6:21-22).

David's worship wasn't about appearances; it was about his unfiltered love for God. Like Florrie's declaration, David's actions remind us that true revival demands vulnerability and authenticity. It's not about how we look or sound; it's about the condition of our hearts.

As the Welsh Revival demonstrated, worship is a catalyst for revival. Singing and heartfelt declarations of faith create an atmosphere where God's Spirit can move freely. In times of revival, worship becomes more than music; it becomes a weapon against darkness, a testimony to God's greatness, and a bridge that connects heaven and earth.

Anointing Jesus' Feet

The story of the sinful woman who anointed Jesus' feet with perfume in Luke 7:36-50 is a powerful illustration of love sparking revival. It begins in the house of Simon the Pharisee, where Jesus was invited to dine. The contrast between Simon's indifferent reception of Jesus and the woman's overwhelming display of love could not be more striking. Simon, a religious leader, offered no water for Jesus' feet, no kiss of greeting, and no oil for His head—customary signs of respect and hospitality in that culture. In contrast, the sinful woman, whose name is not given, approached Jesus with tears streaming down her face, an alabaster jar of perfume in her hands, and a heart overflowing with love and surrender.

This woman was not a stranger to shame. Known in the community for her sinful lifestyle, she must have faced scorn and judgment every time she walked the streets. Yet, when she heard that Jesus was at Simon's house, she came boldly, driven by an irresistible love and longing to be near Him. She stood behind Jesus at His feet, weeping so intensely that her tears wet His feet. With no towel to dry them, she let down her hair—a bold and scandalous act for a woman in her time—and used it to wipe His feet. She kissed His feet repeatedly and anointed them with the costly perfume she had brought.

Every act this woman performed was a declaration of love, humility, and surrender. In that culture, touching someone's feet was an act of profound servitude, and using an expensive perfume showed the depth of her devotion. This wasn't a calculated display meant to gain approval or recognition; it was the unrestrained outpouring of a heart captivated by Jesus. She didn't speak a word, but her actions spoke volumes. They were, in essence, her version of declaring, "I love Jesus Christ with all my heart."

Simon, observing this display, was indignant. He thought to himself, *"If this man were a prophet, He would know who is touching Him and what kind of woman she is—that she is a sinner."* His judgment reveals not only his disdain for the woman but also his limited understanding of who Jesus was. Simon saw only her past, her sins, and her unworthiness, but Jesus saw her heart. Where Simon saw a sinner, Jesus saw a worshiper. Where Simon saw an intrusion, Jesus saw an opportunity to teach a powerful lesson about love and forgiveness.

Jesus, knowing Simon's thoughts, responded with a parable about two debtors. One owed a large sum of money, and the other owed a smaller amount. Neither could repay their debt, so the lender forgave them both. Jesus asked Simon which debtor would love the lender more. Simon reluctantly answered, *"The one who had the bigger debt forgiven."* Jesus affirmed this answer and then turned to the woman, using her actions to illustrate the depth of her love.

"Do you see this woman?" Jesus asked Simon, "I came into your house. You did not give me any water for my feet, but she wet my feet with her tears and wiped them with her hair. You did not give me a kiss, but this woman, from the time I entered, has not stopped kissing my feet. You did not put oil on my head, but she poured perfume on my feet. Therefore, I tell you, her many sins have been forgiven—as her great love has shown. But whoever has been forgiven little loves little."

In this moment, Jesus revealed the essence of revival: a heart fully surrendered to Him, overflowing with love and gratitude. The woman's love wasn't born out of obligation or duty; it was the natural response to the forgiveness and grace she had experienced. She recognized her own unworthiness, but instead of running from Jesus, she ran to Him, offering Him everything she had—her tears, her perfume, her heart.

This story teaches us that revival begins with love. It doesn't matter who you are, what your past looks like, or how the world sees you. What matters is your willingness to come to Jesus, just as you are, and lay everything at His feet. The woman's love for Jesus sparked something not just in her own life but in the hearts of those who witnessed her devotion. Her boldness and surrender became a living testimony of God's grace and the power of forgiveness.

It also highlights the contrast between religious formalism and genuine devotion. Simon, with all his knowledge of the law, missed the opportunity to honor Jesus because his heart was closed. The woman, with no credentials and a tarnished reputation, became a vessel of worship because her heart was open. This is the essence of revival: not programs or rituals but hearts ignited by love for Jesus.

When we love Jesus with all our hearts, as Florrie Evans did, our love has the power to inspire others. Like the woman in Luke 7, our declarations of love don't have to be eloquent or public; they simply need to be real. Whether it's a whisper in prayer, a song of worship, or an act of service, our love for Jesus has the potential to spark a fire that spreads to those around us.

The woman's story reminds us that revival isn't just about what happens in the church; it's about what happens in individual hearts. When we bring our brokenness, our gratitude, and our love to Jesus, He takes it and uses it to ignite something far greater than we could imagine. Her love sparked a moment of revival in Simon's house, challenging everyone present to see Jesus in a new light and to respond with their own acts of worship.

In the same way, your love for Jesus can spark a revival. It doesn't matter if you feel unworthy or overlooked. What matters is your willingness to bring your heart to Him and to declare, with boldness and passion, "I love Jesus Christ with all my heart." Just as the woman's act of love changed the atmosphere in Simon's house, your love can change the atmosphere in your home, your church, and beyond. Revival begins with a heart fully surrendered to God, and it starts with you.

Love and Revival

Let your love spark a revival today. Open your mouth and declare, *"I LOVE JESUS CHRIST – WITH ALL MY HEART."* Let those words flow from a place of complete surrender and watch how God uses them to transform lives. You don't need to be perfect; you just need to be willing. What comes from your mouth could literally change the world.

The revival that began with Florrie Evans didn't end in Wales. It spread across the globe, touching countless lives and leaving a legacy that continues to inspire. The same God who moved in 1904 is moving today, and He's looking for hearts that are ready to spark the next great awakening. Will you be one of them? Will your love for Jesus ignite a fire that transforms the world?

This is your moment. Let your love speak. Let it spark. Let it revive.

6

Intimacy Has Side-Effects

Intimacy with God is a transformational way of life. Those who walk closely with God inevitably exhibit visible side effects that reveal the depth of their relationship with Him. True intimacy isn't something you can hide. It manifests in the choices you make, the words you speak, and the way you carry yourself. It's a fire that burns brightly, drawing others closer to God and setting the standard for a life of faith.

The Visible Marks Of Intimacy

Intimacy with God always leaves a mark. It produces a greater love for Him that overflows into every area of life. This love manifests in increased prayer, heartfelt worship, and a passion for sharing Jesus with others. Those who spend time in the presence of God become more sensitive to His voice and more aligned with His will. Their discernment sharpens, their spiritual gifts come alive, and their hearts are unwilling to entertain gossip, dishonor, or betrayal.

Holiness becomes a defining characteristic of intimacy. To walk closely with God is to walk in purity and obedience. Sin loses its appeal when compared to the beauty of His presence. Intimacy with God compels us to forsake fleshly pleasures and empty pursuits, choosing instead to prioritize His kingdom. The smile of God's presence becomes visible in the lives of those who surrender everything to Him. They radiate peace, joy, and purpose, evidence of a heart fully devoted to the King.

Intimacy Requires Surrender

The cost of intimacy is high. It requires forsaking sin and allowing God to reign on the throne of your life. You cannot serve two masters, as Jesus warned in Matthew 6:24. To draw near to God, you must be willing to let go of anything that competes for His place in your heart. This means surrendering control, abandoning idols, and yielding to His will in every area of life.

True intimacy demands full devotion. Half-hearted attempts won't suffice. God desires all of you—your heart, mind, soul, and strength. This level of surrender can be uncomfortable, but it's also deeply rewarding. When you lay down your life for Him, He fills you with His presence, transforming you from the inside out.

The Fire Of Intimacy

God's presence is often described as a consuming fire. In Exodus 3:2, Moses encountered the burning bush that was ablaze but not consumed. This fire signified God's holiness and His desire to dwell with His people. Similarly, in Acts 2:3, the Holy Spirit descended upon the disciples as tongues of fire, empowering them for ministry.

The fire of intimacy with God doesn't destroy, it purifies. It burns away the impurities in our lives, leaving us refined and ready for His purposes. This fire ignites a passion for holiness and a deep longing to remain close to Him. It's impossible to encounter the fire of God and remain unchanged. His presence transforms everything it touches.

Drawing Near To God

What happened in the Upper Room was totally God. Being in the Upper Room when it happened… that was totally their choice!

The Bible promises that if we draw near to God, He will draw near to us (James 4:8). This invitation is both simple and profound. It requires intentionality, a conscious decision to seek Him daily through prayer, worship, and His Word. It's not about perfection or religious duty but about pursuing a genuine relationship with the Creator.

In Hebrews 10:19-22, believers are encouraged to approach God with confidence, knowing that the blood of Jesus has made a way for us to enter His presence. This boldness comes from understanding that we are loved, forgiven, and invited into a deeper relationship with Him. However, drawing near also requires a willingness to leave behind anything that hinders intimacy.

What Does Intimacy With God Look Like?

Intimacy with God is a lived experience that transforms every aspect of a believer's life. It begins in the secret place, where time is carved out to be alone with Him in prayer, worship, and the study of His Word. This intimacy is cultivated in the quiet moments when the distractions of the world fade, and the heart is wholly focused on Him. It is in these times that God reveals Himself, His nature, and His will, creating a deep connection that cannot be replicated through any other means.

A life marked by intimacy with God exudes peace, even in the midst of chaos. It is not that trials and challenges cease to exist, but there is a steadiness that comes from knowing God is present and in control. This peace transcends understanding and becomes a testimony to others who see it lived out. It is the assurance that comes from walking with the Creator, knowing that nothing can separate us from His love or catch Him by surprise.

Intimacy with God also looks like a heart fully surrendered to His will. It is marked by obedience, not out of duty or fear, but out of love and reverence for who He is. Those who are intimate with God find joy in aligning their lives with His purposes, trusting that His plans are far better than anything they could devise on their own. This surrender often requires letting go of personal ambitions, comforts, and even relationships that hinder a deeper walk with Him.

Worship is a natural overflow of intimacy with God. It is not confined to Sunday services but becomes a lifestyle. Whether through songs of praise, acts of service, or a heart of gratitude, worship becomes the expression of a soul that is captivated by God's goodness. This kind of worship is contagious, drawing others into the presence of God and igniting a hunger in them to know Him more.

A life of intimacy with God is also marked by a love for others that mirrors His own. Those who walk closely with Him carry His heart for people, seeing them as He does—with compassion, grace, and an understanding of their worth. This love moves beyond mere words and into action, meeting needs, offering encouragement, and sharing the hope of Christ with a world in desperate need.

Intimacy with God transforms how we think and speak. The mind is renewed through time spent in His presence, replacing fear, doubt, and negativity with faith, hope, and truth. The words that flow from this renewal are life-giving, edifying others, and pointing them to the Savior. Gossip, criticism, and dishonor have no place in the life of someone who is deeply connected to God.

Perhaps most strikingly, intimacy with God radiates from a person's countenance. There is a noticeable joy and light in those who walk closely with Him. It is as if His presence becomes so intertwined with their being that it spills over into every interaction. This is not something that can be manufactured; it is the natural result of abiding in Him and allowing His Spirit to work in and through them.

Ultimately, intimacy with God looks like a life fully devoted to Him. It is a willingness to go wherever He leads, to do whatever He asks, and to trust Him completely, even when the path is uncertain. It is a journey of drawing ever closer to Him, knowing that the closer we get, the more we reflect His glory to a world that desperately needs to see it.

The Cost Of Following Jesus

Jesus made it clear that following Him would cost us everything. In Matthew 16:24-25 (NKJV), He said, *"If anyone desires to come after Me, let him deny himself, and take up his cross, and follow Me. For whoever desires to save his life will lose it, but whoever loses his life for My sake will find it."*

Intimacy with God requires self-denial and a willingness to carry the cross daily. It's not an easy path, but it's the only one that leads to true life. Those who choose intimacy with God discover a joy and fulfillment that far surpasses anything the world can offer.

The story of Mary and Martha in Luke 10:38-42 illustrates the importance of intimacy with God. While Martha was busy with preparations, Mary chose to sit at Jesus' feet and listen to His teaching. Martha, frustrated by Mary's lack of help, asked Jesus to intervene. But Jesus gently rebuked her, saying, "Martha, Martha, you are worried and upset about many things, but only one thing is necessary. Mary has chosen what is better, and it will not be taken away from her."

Mary's choice to prioritize intimacy with Jesus over busyness is a powerful reminder for us today. Like Martha, we can become consumed by the demands of life, but true fulfillment comes from sitting at His feet. Intimacy with God is the "one thing" that matters most.

While intimacy with God comes at a cost, the rewards far outweigh the sacrifices. His presence fills us with joy, His peace steadies us in trials, and His love transforms every part of our lives. Intimacy with God unlocks spiritual power, fuels our passion for His kingdom, and equips us to make an eternal impact.

The smile of God's presence becomes our greatest treasure. It's a joy that cannot be replicated by anything else in this world. Those who walk closely with Him experience a depth of love and purpose that sustains them through every season.

Will You Choose Intimacy?

The choice to pursue intimacy with God is yours. He invites you to draw near, to surrender everything, and to experience the side effects of a life fully devoted to Him. The question is, will you accept the invitation?

Intimacy with God changes everything. It transforms your heart, renews your mind, and equips you to live a life of impact. The side effects are undeniable; greater love, holiness, power, and joy. They are the marks of a life that has encountered the living God.

So, take the step. Seek Him with all your heart. Let His fire refine you, His presence fill you, and His love compel you. The cost is high, but the reward is eternal. Choose intimacy and watch as God uses your life to reveal His glory.

7

Don't Be Caught Asleep!

Jesus' warnings about spiritual unpreparedness are piercing and clear. In His parable of the ten virgins, He highlights that many who appear ready will, in truth, be unprepared for His return. They will be distracted, spiritually drowsy, and lacking the genuine intimacy with God necessary to sustain them through the wait. This message is a wake-up call for every believer to examine their walk with God. Revival is a divine alarm meant to awaken the hearts of His people.

Will we be found faithful, or will we be caught asleep?

The Parable Of The Ten Virgins: A Call To Readiness

The parable of the ten virgins in Matthew 25:1-13 is one of Jesus' most vivid and impactful teachings on spiritual readiness. It paints a picture of anticipation, urgency, and the consequences of unpreparedness. The story unfolds with ten virgins eagerly awaiting the arrival of the bridegroom. Each carries a lamp, symbolizing their role and readiness to meet him. But the distinction between the wise and the foolish lies not in their outward appearance or actions but in their preparation—or lack thereof.

All ten virgins had lamps, but only five brought extra oil. The bridegroom's arrival was delayed, and as the night wore on, all of them fell asleep. At midnight, the cry rang out: "Here's the bridegroom! Come out to meet him!" The wise virgins, prepared for the unexpected delay, quickly trimmed their lamps and lit them with the extra oil they had brought. The foolish virgins, however, found their lamps flickering and running out of fuel. In desperation, they begged the wise for some of their oil, but there wasn't enough to share. The foolish virgins rushed off to find oil, but while they were gone, the bridegroom arrived, and the door to the wedding feast was shut. When they returned and pleaded for entry, they were met with the somber words: *"I do not know you."*

The power of this parable lies in its profound simplicity. All ten virgins looked the part. They were dressed for the occasion, carried lamps, and shared the same anticipation for the bridegroom's arrival. To an outsider, there was no visible difference between them until the crucial moment of testing. The midnight cry revealed what had been hidden: five were prepared, and five were not. Their outward appearance meant nothing when it came to their readiness to meet the bridegroom.

The oil in this parable symbolizes intimacy with God, an inner reservoir of faith, devotion, and spiritual sustenance cultivated through consistent time in His presence. The wise virgins understood the importance of this oil. They knew that the bridegroom's arrival might be delayed, and that endurance required preparation. Their extra oil represented a thriving relationship with God, one that sustained them even in the waiting.

In stark contrast, the foolish virgins underestimated the significance of preparation. They assumed that their lamps would be enough or that they could rely on the readiness of others. This assumption proved disastrous. When the moment of truth arrived, their lack of oil left them scrambling, unprepared, and ultimately excluded. The sobering reality is that the oil cannot be borrowed. Intimacy with God is deeply personal and non-transferable. It requires daily cultivation through prayer, worship, and obedience.

This parable challenges us to evaluate the state of our own lamps. Are we wise or foolish in our approach to spiritual readiness? Are we diligently maintaining our relationship with God, ensuring that we have the 'extra oil' needed to endure delays, trials, and uncertainties? Or are we neglecting our spiritual lives, assuming that surface-level faith will be enough when the time comes?

The midnight cry is a wake-up call. It reminds us that the bridegroom's arrival, that is Jesus' return, is both certain and unpredictable. The delay in His coming tests the faithfulness of His followers. Will we grow complacent, allowing our lamps to run dry? Or will we remain vigilant, keeping our lamps filled and our hearts ready? The wise virgins demonstrate the importance of being prepared at all times. They show us that spiritual readiness is not a one-time decision but a daily commitment to walk closely with God.

The response of the bridegroom to the foolish virgins is one of the most chilling aspects of this parable. When they plead for entry, he replies, "I do not know you." These words reveal the heart of the issue: the lack of relationship. The foolish virgins had the outward appearance of readiness, but their failure to cultivate intimacy with the bridegroom left them unrecognizable to him. This is a sobering reminder that participation in religious activities, good reputations, and outward appearances mean nothing if they are not rooted in a genuine, thriving relationship with Jesus.

The lesson here is clear: spiritual readiness cannot be borrowed or postponed. It must be cultivated daily. The oil of intimacy with God is what sustains us, fuels our lamps, and prepares us for His return. It is what enables us to endure delays and remain faithful in the waiting. Without this oil, our lamps may look good on the outside, but they will lack the light needed to guide us into the wedding feast.

Jesus' parable is a call to live with urgency and purpose in the present. The midnight cry could come at any moment. Will you be ready? This is not a question of fear but of love and devotion. Those who carry the extra oil are not motivated by a sense of obligation but by a deep longing to be with the bridegroom. Their preparation is an act of love, a response to His worthiness.

In light of this parable, we are invited to examine our own lives. Are we carrying extra oil, ensuring that our spiritual lives are sustained no matter the delay? Are we investing in our relationship with God, or are we hoping to scrape by on borrowed faith and last-minute efforts?

The time to prepare is now. The bridegroom is coming. Will your lamp be ready to shine brightly when He arrives?

What Does It Mean to Carry Oil?

Carrying oil is about living in a state of constant readiness. It's a commitment to prioritize your relationship with God above all else. The wise virgins understood the bridegroom's arrival might be delayed, so they prepared for the long haul. Their extra oil symbolized a thriving relationship with God, cultivated through consistent devotion. They were not caught off guard when the call came because they had already done the work of preparation.

On the other hand, the foolish virgins represent those who neglect their spiritual lives. They focus on appearances and surface-level engagement with God but lack the inner substance of intimacy. When the moment of truth arrives, their lack of oil is exposed, and they find themselves unprepared.

There are things we must buy but not with money. In Acts 8:20 Peter said the gift of God cannot be bought with money. You cannot buy this oil with money. The oil cannot be borrowed because intimacy with

God is personal and non-transferable. It requires time, effort, and surrender. The real cost is of the heart not the wallet. Not something we can spare, but something that will require our life.

God provides the oil, but it is our responsibility to draw on it and steward it. A thriving spiritual life requires consistent prayer, study of His Word, and worship. It means seeking Him not out of obligation but out of love. The wise understand that the wait may be long, but their devotion keeps their lamps burning. The foolish, however, live for the moment, neglecting their relationship with God until it's too late.

Faithfulness Is Non-Negotiable

When Jesus asks in Luke 18:8, *"When the Son of Man comes, will He find faith on the earth?"* He is pointing to the kind of faith that goes beyond words or fleeting emotions. True faith is demonstrated in faithfulness—a life marked by consistent devotion to God. This faithfulness is not about perfection but perseverance. It's about showing up daily to seek God, even when it's hard or inconvenient.

Faithfulness requires commitment. It means staying connected to God through prayer, worship, and obedience, even when the world offers distractions and temptations. The wise virgins were faithful in their preparation. They didn't wait for the bridegroom's arrival to start gathering oil; they lived in readiness. The foolish virgins, however, represent those who neglect their relationship with God until it's too late. They assume they'll have time to catch up, but when the moment comes, their unpreparedness costs them everything.

Revival is a lifestyle of faithfulness. It's about living in a state of anticipation, ready for God to move at any moment. The wise understand that faithfulness is non-negotiable. They keep their lamps full and their hearts aligned with God, knowing that His return is certain, even if the timing is unknown.

God Provides The Oil And The Fire

The imagery of the lamp, oil, and flame in the parable is profound. The lamp represents the believer's life, the oil symbolizes the Holy Spirit, and the flame is the light of God's presence. God provides both the oil and the fire, but we are called to be the wick—the connection between heaven and earth. The wick draws the oil into the flame, sustaining the light. Without the wick, the lamp cannot burn. Without the oil, the wick burns out. Our role is to remain in place, fully surrendered to God, allowing His presence to flow through us.

The foolish virgins' failure was not in owning lamps but in neglecting the oil. They misunderstood the importance of connection. They relied on appearances and association, assuming it would be enough. But when the bridegroom came, their lack of oil revealed their lack of relationship. The wise, however, were prepared. Their lamps were ready, their wicks trimmed, and their oil sufficient.

God is faithful to provide the oil and the fire, but He asks us to steward it well. Are you drawing deeply from His presence, allowing His oil to sustain your flame? Or are you running on empty, hoping to catch up later? The time to prepare is now.

Noah's Ark

The story of Noah and the ark is a timeless reminder of the critical importance of preparation and faithfulness. It mirrors the themes of readiness and obedience found in the parable of the ten virgins. In Genesis 6, God revealed His plan to flood the earth in response to the wickedness of humanity. Yet, amid this impending judgment, Noah found favor with God because of his righteousness and faithfulness. God instructed Noah to build an ark, a massive vessel that would serve as the means of salvation for him, his family, and the animals God would preserve.

Noah's task was monumental, both in scale and in the faith it required. Building an ark of such size, especially in a land where rain was a foreign concept, must have seemed foolish to onlookers. Day after day, as Noah and his family worked on the ark, they likely faced ridicule and disbelief from those around them. "What are you doing, Noah? Why waste your life on something so absurd?" they might have said. But Noah's unwavering obedience to God's instructions set him apart. He trusted God's word, even when it seemed improbable or irrational, and his faithfulness became the key to his survival.

For years, Noah labored in faith. Every nail driven into the ark was an act of trust in God's promises. Every plank placed was a declaration of belief in what God had spoken. He did not waver, even though the skies remained clear and the earth seemed as stable as ever. Noah understood that preparation was not about what seemed immediately necessary but about aligning with God's timeline and purposes. His obedience was a demonstration of his deep relationship with God, a relationship rooted in trust and reverence.

When the rains finally came, they came suddenly and without reprieve. The fountains of the deep burst forth, and the heavens opened. In that moment, it became clear that Noah's preparation had not been in vain. The ark was complete, and God Himself shut the door, sealing Noah and his family inside. For those outside the ark, the time for preparation had passed. The warnings they had ignored, the mockery they had hurled, and the opportunities they had squandered were now painfully evident. Like the foolish virgins in Jesus' parable, they found themselves unprepared for the reality that had arrived.

The parallels between Noah's story and the parable of the ten virgins are striking. Both narratives emphasize the importance of readiness and the dire consequences of neglecting it. Just as the foolish virgins assumed they had time to acquire oil, the people in Noah's day assumed they had time to continue their routines. They carried on with their lives, ignoring the signs and warnings, until the moment of reckoning arrived. And by then, it was too late.

Noah's story also highlights the personal nature of preparation. Building the ark was not something Noah could delegate or outsource. It required his full involvement, his labor, and his dedication. In the same way, cultivating a relationship with God and being spiritually prepared is a deeply personal responsibility. It cannot be borrowed or transferred from someone else. Just as the wise virgins could not share their oil, Noah could not bring anyone onto the ark who had not chosen to align themselves with God's plan. The choice to prepare is an individual act of faith.

Preparation is not just about foresight; it is an act of faith and trust in God's promises. It is a declaration that we believe what God has spoken, even when the evidence is not immediately visible. Noah's faithfulness ensured the survival of his family and the continuation of life on earth. Like the wise virgins, Noah demonstrates that readiness is not about reacting to the last-minute cry but about living a life of consistent obedience and faithfulness.

The lesson for us is clear: we are called to build our spiritual ark through prayer, worship, and obedience. Just as Noah prepared for the flood, we must prepare for the return of Christ and the fulfillment of God's promises. This preparation cannot be half-hearted or delayed. It requires diligence, focus, and a commitment to prioritize God above all else. The distractions and temptations of the world may seek to pull us away, but we must remain steadfast, trusting that our labor in faith is not in vain.

Noah's story also reminds us of God's faithfulness. Just as God provided Noah with the blueprint for the ark and the means to build it, He provides us with everything we need for spiritual readiness. He has given us His Word, His Spirit, and His presence to guide and sustain us. Our responsibility is to respond with faith and obedience, trusting that God's plans are perfect and His promises are sure.

As we reflect on the story of Noah and the parable of the ten virgins, we are reminded that the time to prepare is now. The rains came suddenly in Noah's day, and the midnight cry came unexpectedly in Jesus' parable. In both cases, the opportunity to prepare had an expiration date. Let us not be like the foolish virgins or the people in Noah's day who were caught unprepared. Instead, let us be diligent, building our spiritual ark and keeping our lamps filled with the oil of intimacy with God. The door to the ark will not remain open forever. Will you be ready when it closes?

Revival As God's Wake-Up Call

Revival is God's way of shaking His people awake, calling them to realign with His purposes. It's not just about emotional experiences or temporary enthusiasm, it's about lasting transformation. Revival asks the question: Are you awake yet? Are you prepared to meet God, not just in a moment of worship but in every aspect of your life?

The wise understand that revival flames are sustained by the oil of intimacy. They are the ones who remain faithful, drawing deeply from their relationship with God to keep their lamps burning. The foolish, however, miss the opportunity because they wait too long to prepare. When the moment comes, they find themselves outside, knocking on a door that will not open.

Revival is both a warning and an invitation. It's a call to examine your heart, repent of distractions, and draw closer to God. Don't be caught asleep in the midst of a great awakening. Let the oil of His presence fill your lamp, and let your flame burn brightly for His glory.

The time to prepare is now. Will you be ready?

8

The Dress Rehearsal

Revival is God's urgent wake-up call to His church, a time to prepare for the ultimate celebration of Christ's return. Like a bride eagerly readying herself for her wedding day, revival is the spiritual dress rehearsal that urges believers to align their hearts, lives, and worship with the coming King. It is a season where God's presence flows abundantly, reminding His people to stay awake, remain faithful, and be ready for His return. This preparation is essential for those who long to see Him face to face.

Revival serves as a divine alarm clock, shaking the church out of spiritual complacency and slumber. It is God's way of crying out to His people: *"Jesus is coming back soon! Are you awake? Are you ready?"* Romans 13:11 captures this urgency: *"The hour has come for you to wake up from your slumber, because our salvation is nearer now than when we first believed."* Revival compels us to examine our hearts, casting aside distractions and sins that so easily entangle us. It is a time to renew our devotion, align with God's will, and embrace the calling to live in anticipation of Christ's return.

This wake-up call is not for the faint-hearted. Revival often exposes the areas of our lives that need refining, calling us to repentance and a deeper surrender to God's purpose. It reminds us that Jesus' return is not a distant event but an imminent reality. The church must respond with urgency, understanding that revival is not just for personal renewal but a preparation for the harvest and the final fulfillment of God's plan.

A Dress Rehearsal For Eternity

The imagery of a wedding rehearsal perfectly illustrates the purpose of revival. Just as a bride meticulously prepares every detail for her wedding day, the church must prepare itself for the return of the Bridegroom, Jesus Christ. Revival is the season where God pours out His Spirit, ensuring His people are adorned in holiness, faithfulness, and readiness for the great celebration to come.

Consider the words of Jesus in Luke 12:35-36: *"Be dressed ready for service and keep your lamps burning, like servants waiting for their master to return from a wedding banquet, so that when he comes and knocks they can immediately open the door for him."* Revival calls us to be spiritually dressed and ready, with our lamps burning brightly. This is not the time to scramble for oil at the last minute but to remain steadfast in worship, prayer, and faithfulness.

Revival also mirrors the parable of the great banquet in Luke 14:16-24, where a master invites many guests to a feast, only to be met with excuses. The master's response is to open the invitation to anyone willing to come. Revival is this open invitation—a chance to enter into God's presence, experience His glory, and prepare for the ultimate feast. However, it requires a response. Just as the invited guests missed their opportunity due to distraction, so too can believers miss the move of God if they remain unprepared.

Marriage Imagery In The Bible: The Covenant Relationship Between God And His People

Marriage imagery is one of the most profound ways the Bible illustrates the relationship between God and His people. From the Old

Testament to the New, this metaphor communicates covenant love, faithfulness, and intimacy. Just as a husband and wife enter into a lifelong union, God enters into an unbreakable covenant with His people, calling them to be His treasured possession and bride. This imagery not only emphasizes the depth of God's love but also sets the stage for revival as a season of preparation for the ultimate union with Christ at His return.

In the Old Testament, God often refers to Israel as His bride, expressing both His unwavering love and His heartache when His people turn away. For example, in Hosea, God uses the prophet's marriage to an unfaithful wife as a symbol of His relationship with Israel. Hosea's relentless pursuit of his wife, despite her unfaithfulness, reflects God's enduring love and mercy. *"I will betroth you to me forever; I will betroth you in righteousness and justice, in love and compassion."* (Hosea 2:19). This imagery reveals that God's covenant is not dependent on human perfection but on His unchanging love and commitment. Revival, then, is a call for the bride to return to her first love, to renew the vows of faithfulness, and to enter into deeper intimacy with her divine Bridegroom.

The New Testament carries this theme forward, presenting the church as the bride of Christ. In Ephesians 5:25-27, Paul writes, *"Husbands, love your wives, just as Christ loved the church and gave himself up for her to make her holy, cleansing her by the washing with water through the word, and to present her to himself as a radiant church, without stain or wrinkle or any other blemish, but holy and blameless."* This passage not only highlights Christ's sacrificial love but also underscores the church's role in preparing for His return. Revival is like the bride's dress rehearsal, a time to cleanse, purify, and adorn herself with righteousness in anticipation of the wedding feast of the Lamb.

Jesus Himself uses marriage imagery to describe His return and the kingdom of heaven. In the parable of the ten virgins (Matthew 25:1-13), the focus is on readiness. The wise virgins, with their lamps full of oil, represent those who have cultivated intimacy with God and are prepared for the Bridegroom's arrival. The foolish virgins, lacking oil, symbolize those who have neglected their relationship with God and find themselves unprepared when the moment comes. This parable ties directly into the concept of revival as a wake-up call, urging the church to stay spiritually vigilant and ensure their hearts are filled with the oil of His presence.

Revelation provides the ultimate culmination of this marriage imagery, portraying the union between Christ and His church as the marriage supper of the Lamb. Revelation 19:7-9 declares, *"Let us rejoice and be glad and give him glory! For the wedding of the Lamb has come, and his bride has made herself ready. Fine linen, bright and clean, was given her to wear."* The fine linen represents the righteous acts of God's people, prepared through seasons of revival and faithfulness. This passage reminds us that revival is not an end in itself but a preparation for the eternal celebration where the Bridegroom and His bride will dwell together forever.

Revival also reflects the deep longing of God's heart for His people. Just as a bridegroom yearns for his bride, God desires an intimate relationship with His church. Isaiah 62:5 captures this beautifully: *"As a bridegroom rejoices over his bride, so will your God rejoice over you."* Revival is a time when the church responds to that longing, stepping away from worldly distractions and recommitting to the covenant of love and holiness. It is a season of rekindled passion, where worship becomes the song of the bride's heart, echoing her devotion to the Bridegroom.

However, marriage imagery in the Bible also comes with a solemn warning. Just as a bride is called to faithfulness, so too must the church remain loyal to Christ. James 4:4 starkly warns, *"You adulterous people, don't you know that friendship with the world means enmity against*

God?" Revival is a call to forsake all other loves, to tear down the idols that compete for our affection, and to return wholeheartedly to our divine Husband. It is a time of choosing—choosing God's kingdom over the world, His righteousness over sin, and His presence over comfort.

The cost of this faithfulness is great, but the reward is eternal. Revelation 21:2-3 offers a breathtaking vision of the bride's future: *"I saw the Holy City, the new Jerusalem, coming down out of heaven from God, prepared as a bride beautifully dressed for her husband. And I heard a loud voice from the throne saying, 'Look! God's dwelling place is now among the people, and he will dwell with them. They will be his people, and God himself will be with them and be their God.'"*
Revival is the anticipation of this moment—a foretaste of the joy and glory to come.

In this light, revival is both an invitation and a challenge. It invites the church to step into her role as the bride of Christ, to prepare her heart and life for the wedding day. It challenges believers to forsake complacency, to fill their lamps with oil, and to live in expectation of the Bridegroom's return. Just as a bride invests time, energy, and care into every detail of her wedding, the church must pour her heart into preparing for the ultimate celebration.

Marriage imagery in the Bible reminds us that revival is not just about emotional experiences or numerical growth; it is about restoring the covenant relationship between God and His people. It is a time to fall in love with Jesus all over again, to declare with passion and conviction, "I am my beloved's, and my beloved is mine" (Song of Solomon 6:3). Let revival spark the cry of the bride's heart, readying the church for the day when the Bridegroom will come, and the eternal union will begin.

The Patience of God

One of the most beautiful aspects of revival is its reflection of God's patience and mercy. As 2 Peter 3:9 reminds us, *"The Lord is not slow in keeping his promise, as some understand slowness. Instead, he is patient with you, not wanting anyone to perish, but everyone to come to repentance."* Revival is an extension of this patience—a season where God gives His people the opportunity to turn back to Him, align their lives with His purposes, and prepare for His return.

This patience should not be mistaken for leniency. Revival is a time of urgency, a call to action that requires a response. It is God's way of ensuring that no one has an excuse when the final harvest comes. Just as the harvest is the culmination of a season of growth, revival is the spiritual harvest where God gathers those who have been faithful.

Revival as a Time of Refreshing

Acts 3:19-20 describes revival as a *"time of refreshing from the Lord."* This refreshing is not just physical or emotional—it is a deep spiritual renewal that awakens the church to its purpose. Revival restores what has been lost, breaks chains of bondage, and ignites a passion for holiness and evangelism. It is a foretaste of heaven, a glimpse of the glory that awaits those who remain faithful.

This time of refreshing is also a call to action. Revival is not a passive experience but an active participation in God's kingdom work. It equips believers to share the Gospel, serve their communities, and live as ambassadors of Christ. It is a season where God's Spirit moves powerfully, breaking through barriers and transforming lives.

The ultimate purpose of revival is to prepare the church for the return of Christ. As 1 Thessalonians 4:16-18 describes, the Lord will descend from heaven with a loud command, and the dead in Christ will rise first. Those who are still alive will be caught up with them to meet the Lord in the air. Revival is the dress rehearsal for this glorious event—a time to ensure we are awake, ready, and fully devoted to Him.

Jesus Himself warned in Luke 12:40, *"You also must be ready, because the Son of Man will come at an hour when you do not expect him."* Revival is the opportunity to heed this warning, to align our lives with God's purposes, and to live in expectation of His return. It is a time to renew our commitment, strengthen our faith, and ensure that our lamps are burning brightly.

Embracing the Call

Revival is a divine invitation to prepare for eternity. It is a time to evaluate our hearts, renew our devotion, and align our lives with God's purposes. It is the dress rehearsal for the greatest celebration of all: the return of the King.

As we pray for revival, may we embrace it with open hearts and willing spirits. Let us not miss the opportunity to be part of God's movement, to experience His power and presence, and to prepare for the day when we will see Him face to face.

The time is now—wake up, lift your head, and step into the rehearsal for eternity.

9

Revival Is Costly But Affordable

Revival is one of the greatest gifts God offers to His people. It breathes new life into weary souls, restores broken relationships, and reawakens a church that has grown stagnant. But as glorious as revival is, it comes with a cost. It demands full surrender, unwavering faith, and a willingness to let go of old habits and comfort zones. It is costly, yes, but never unaffordable to those who hunger and thirst for God. For those who truly desire His presence, the cost pales in comparison to the riches of His glory.

The Samaritan Revival: Revival Lingers Where People Linger

The Samaritan Revival is one of the most striking examples of how a single encounter with Jesus can transform not just an individual but an entire community. Found in John 4, this story begins with a woman burdened by shame, ostracized from her society, and coming to the well at an unusual hour to avoid others. Yet, this is precisely where Jesus met her—at her point of need and longing. Their conversation wasn't just about water; it was about life, redemption, and worship. Jesus, knowing her heart and her past, offered her the living water that would forever quench her spiritual thirst.

The woman's reaction was nothing short of extraordinary. The same woman who avoided others now boldly proclaimed her testimony to the very people who once shunned her. *"Come, see a man who told me every-*

thing I ever did. Could this be the Messiah?" she exclaimed (John 4:29). Her courage and transparency were fueled by her encounter with Jesus, and her words carried the power of her transformation. She became a catalyst for revival, showing that even the least likely among us can be used mightily by God.

What followed was a ripple effect of revival. The townspeople, stirred by the woman's testimony, left their routines and came to meet Jesus. This was not a casual gathering; they came with an expectation and a hunger to know if He truly was the Messiah. When they encountered Jesus for themselves, their initial intrigue turned into faith. They no longer relied solely on the woman's testimony but declared, *"Now we believe, not because of what you said, but because we have heard Him ourselves and know that this man really is the Savior of the world"* (John 4:42).

What made this revival unique was not just the initial spark but its continuation. The people's hunger for more led them to ask Jesus to stay, and He obliged, remaining with them for two days. This extended time of teaching, fellowship, and revelation brought about even greater transformation. Many more believed because the townspeople lingered in Jesus' presence. Their willingness to make room for Him, to set aside their schedules and routines, created the fertile ground for revival to flourish.

This account reveals a profound truth about revival: it lingers where people linger. Revival does not come to the hurried or the half-hearted; it comes to those who prioritize God's presence above all else. The Samaritans were willing to disrupt their lives, to leave their comfort zones, and to devote themselves entirely to Jesus. They teach us that revival requires intentionality—it demands that we slow down, wait on God, and open our hearts to His work.

Imagine, for a moment, if the Samaritan woman had kept silent. What if she had allowed her shame or fear of rejection to prevent her from sharing her encounter? The entire city might have missed its moment of awakening. Similarly, imagine if the townspeople had dismissed her testimony as mere excitement or emotion. What if they had been too busy or uninterested to come to Jesus? The revival that transformed Samaria would never have taken place.

This is a sobering reminder for us today. How often do we let distractions, busyness, or skepticism prevent us from experiencing the fullness of God's presence? How often do we rush through our moments with Him, failing to linger in prayer, worship, or His Word? Revival is not something we can manufacture or schedule. It is a move of God that comes when hearts are fully open and willing to make room for Him.

The story of the Samaritan revival challenges us to examine our hunger for God. Are we truly desperate for His presence, or have we grown complacent? Revival begins with individuals who, like the Samaritan woman, are transformed by an encounter with Jesus and are willing to share their testimony boldly. It spreads when communities, like the Samaritans, set aside their distractions and prioritize God above all else.

This revival demonstrates the inclusiveness of God's kingdom. The Samaritans were a marginalized group, often despised by the Jews. Yet, Jesus chose to reveal Himself to them in a profound way, breaking cultural and societal barriers. This reminds us that revival is not confined to specific places, people, or traditions. It can happen anywhere and among anyone who is willing to seek God with all their heart.

The Samaritan revival also teaches us the importance of sustaining revival. It's not enough to have a single encounter or a fleeting experience of God's presence. Revival requires perseverance and a continual hunger for more of Him. The Samaritans could have been content with their initial meeting with Jesus, but instead, they begged Him to stay. This lingering, this desire to go deeper, is what kept the revival alive and brought about lasting change.

As we reflect on this story, let it stir within us a longing for the same kind of revival. Let us be like the Samaritan woman, unashamed to declare what Jesus has done for us. Let us be like the townspeople, willing to set aside everything to pursue Him. And let us remember that revival lingers where people linger. May we create space in our lives and in our churches for God to move, trusting that He will meet us in ways that exceed our expectations. Revival is costly; it requires time, devotion, and surrender, but it is ALWAYS worth it.

The Cost Of Revival: Surrender And Repentance

When you study church history you will easily discover... the most significant catalyst for revival since the birth of the church has been when a people humbled themselves, sought the Lord, and worshipped Him. Revival always carries a cost, but the price is one of spiritual surrender rather than material wealth. It demands that we give God every part of our lives, holding nothing back. It calls us to repentance, humility, and the intentional choice to let go of anything that separates us from His presence. Revival cannot take root in hearts that cling to sin or remain entangled in worldly distractions. It grows in the soil of brokenness, watered by prayers of repentance and cultivated by a desire to see God glorified above all else.

The promise of revival is beautifully articulated in 2 Chronicles 7:14: *"If My people, who are called by My name, will humble themselves and pray and seek My face and turn from their wicked ways, then I will hear from heaven, and I will forgive their sin and heal their land."* This verse highlights the conditions of revival—humility, prayer, and repentance. WHO is being addressed here? Not the world, but the people of

God. Those who are called according to His name! Revival is sparked by the people of God.

It begins when we bow low before God, acknowledging our need for His mercy, and seek Him with undivided hearts. Turning from sin is not optional; it is the foundation of any true revival. God will not pour His Spirit into vessels unwilling to be cleansed.

A striking biblical example of the cost of revival is found in the story of King Josiah in 2 Kings 22-23. Josiah came to power during a time of spiritual decay in Judah. Idolatry was rampant, and the people had drifted far from God's commandments. When Josiah was just 26 years old, a profound moment occurred: the Book of the Law was discovered in the temple. As the words of God's covenant were read to him, Josiah was overcome with grief. He tore his robes as a sign of deep repentance, recognizing the gravity of the nation's sin and how far they had fallen from God's ways.

Josiah's response to the revelation of God's Word was not passive. He immediately took action, leading the nation into a sweeping revival. He ordered the destruction of idols, altars, and high places dedicated to false gods. He removed the priests who had led the people into idolatry and restored the temple as a place of true worship. Josiah renewed the covenant between God and the people, committing himself and the nation to walk in obedience to the Lord's commands.

This revival came at a great cost. Josiah faced resistance from those who were comfortable with their idolatrous ways. The reforms he instituted disrupted the status quo and likely angered powerful individuals who profited from the nation's sin. Revival always challenges complacency, comfort, and the systems that perpetuate spiritual stagnation. Josiah's courage in confronting sin, even at great personal and political risk, demonstrates the boldness required to bring about lasting spiritual renewal.

The story of Josiah reveals another key aspect of revival: it begins with the leader but spreads to the community. Josiah's personal repentance and commitment to God ignited a collective turning back to the Lord. This is true for us today. Revival often starts in the heart of one person who is willing to pay the cost of surrender and repentance. As that fire spreads, it draws others into the transforming work of God.

But let us not overlook the personal cost involved in revival. To surrender completely to God means laying down our pride, confessing our sins, and allowing Him to reshape our lives. It is a deeply humbling process, one that requires us to confront the areas of our hearts that we would rather ignore. Like Josiah, we must allow God's Word to cut through our defenses and reveal the truth about our spiritual condition. This is not an easy or comfortable process, but it is necessary for true revival.

Revival also demands a willingness to confront the sin in the world around us. Josiah's reforms were not limited to his personal life; they extended to the entire nation. He tore down idols, silenced false prophets, and reestablished true worship. This demonstrates that revival is not only about personal transformation but also about bringing God's kingdom to bear in every sphere of life. It is a call to stand against injustice, to reject the idols of our culture, and to proclaim the truth of God's Word with boldness.

The cost of revival may seem high, but the reward is immeasurable. For Josiah and the people of Judah, revival brought spiritual renewal, restored worship, and a renewed covenant with God. For us, the fruit of revival includes a deeper relationship with God, a greater sensitivity to His Spirit, and the joy of seeing lives transformed by His power. While the process of repentance and surrender may be painful, the outcome is a life that reflects God's glory and a heart that burns with passion for Him.

Imagine what could happen if we embraced the cost of revival in our own lives. What if we, like Josiah, allowed God's Word to pierce our hearts and expose the sin that needs to be uprooted? What if we were willing to destroy the idols that have taken His place in our hearts, whether they be comfort, success, or approval? What if we chose to prioritize God's presence above everything else, no matter the cost?

Revival is not out of reach; it is a promise waiting to be fulfilled in the lives of those who are willing to pay the price!

As we reflect on the story of Josiah, let it inspire us to take the steps necessary for revival in our own lives and communities. Let us humble ourselves, seek God's face, and turn from our wicked ways. Let us confront the sin in our lives and in the world around us with courage and conviction. And let us trust that God, in His faithfulness, will hear from heaven, forgive our sin, and heal our land. The cost of revival is great, but it is never greater than the joy of experiencing God's presence and the transformation that only He can bring.

New Wine Requires New Wineskins

Jesus' teaching about new wine and new wineskins in Luke 5:37-38 is a fitting metaphor for revival. He explains that new wine cannot be poured into old wineskins because the skins will burst, ruining both the wine and the container. Instead, new wine must be poured into fresh wineskins that can expand with it.

Revival is like new wine; fresh, dynamic, and transformative. It cannot be contained in old mindsets, rigid traditions, or inflexible structures. It demands that we embrace change and let go of anything that restricts the Spirit's movement. This can be uncomfortable, even painful. It requires us to stretch, to grow, and to release our grip on the familiar.

Many resist revival because it disrupts their comfort zones. Like the Pharisees, they cling to their traditions and routines, unwilling to make room for God's new work. But revival exposes these old wineskins for what they are, insufficient to carry the weight of God's glory. It calls us to embrace new wineskins, to be flexible and open to the Spirit's leading.

Are you willing to let God reshape you into a new wineskin? Are you willing to let go of old habits, preferences, and comforts to receive His new wine? Revival demands that we do. It is costly, but the reward is worth it.

The Disruptive Nature Of Revival

Revival is not neat or predictable. It disrupts our routines, challenges our priorities, and demands our attention. It shakes us out of complacency and forces us to confront the state of our hearts. This disruption is not meant to harm us but to awaken us to the fullness of life in Christ.

Consider the Day of Pentecost in Acts 2. When the Holy Spirit descended on the disciples, it was anything but quiet. A sound like a rushing wind filled the room, tongues of fire rested on each person, and they began speaking in other languages. The noise and commotion drew a crowd, and Peter preached with boldness, leading 3,000 people to salvation that day.

Pentecost was disruptive, but it was also transformative. It marked the birth of the church and the beginning of a global movement. Revival today carries the same disruptive power. It challenges us to let go of our comfort zones and step into the unknown, trusting God to lead us. It calls us to action, to boldness, and to a renewed sense of purpose.

Are you willing to let revival disrupt your life?
Are you willing to let it challenge your routines and reshape your priorities?

Revival demands that we do. It is not comfortable, but it is life-changing.

The Presence Of God: The Heart Of Revival

At the center of every revival is the presence of God. Without His presence, there can be no revival. It is His Spirit that brings life, transformation, and power. Revival begins when we seek Him with all our hearts, prioritizing His presence above all else.

Moses understood this when he said, *"If Your Presence does not go with us, do not send us up from here."* (Exodus 33:15). He knew that without God's presence, their journey would be meaningless. The same is true for us. Revival is not about programs or strategies; it is about creating space for God to move.

In Acts 3:19, Peter calls the people to repentance, saying, *"Repent, then, and turn to God, so that your sins may be wiped out, that times of refreshing may come from the Lord."* These times of refreshing come only from being in God's presence. They are the essence of revival—a renewal of our spirits, a rekindling of our passion, and a deepening of our relationship with Him.

Revival Is Affordable To The Hungry

While revival is costly, it is never out of reach for those who hunger and thirst for God. In Matthew 5:6, Jesus says, *"Blessed are those who hunger and thirst for righteousness, for they will be filled."* Hunger is the key to revival. It draws us to God, compels us to seek Him, and opens the door for His Spirit to move.

Hunger for God is what drives people to pray fervently, to worship passionately, and to repent wholeheartedly. It is what keeps us lingering in His presence, refusing to leave until we encounter Him. Hunger makes revival not only possible but inevitable.

Are you hungry for revival? Are you willing to pay the price of surrender, repentance, and devotion? Revival is costly, but it is always affordable to those who truly desire it. If you hunger for God, He will fill you. If you seek Him, you will find Him. And if you welcome His Spirit, He will bring revival to your life and your community.

Revival is God's invitation to experience more of Him. It is a call to deeper intimacy, greater faith, and a renewed sense of purpose. It is costly, yes, but it is a cost worth paying. Will you accept the invitation? Will you pay the price?

The choice is yours.

10

Pentecost Is For Everyone

Pentecost stands as one of the most pivotal events in Christian history, yet it often carries misconceptions about its significance. For some, Pentecost is seen as an exclusive hallmark of a specific denomination or tradition. But the truth is, Pentecost is not the property of Pentecostals, it is a divine gift for every believer who seeks the fullness of God's Spirit. It was at Pentecost that the church was birthed, and the promise of the Holy Spirit was fulfilled. This chapter explores how Pentecost invites all believers into a Spirit-filled life marked by power, purpose, and revival.

The invitation of Pentecost is universal. In Acts 2:4, the Scripture says, *"All of them were filled with the Holy Spirit and began to speak in other tongues as the Spirit enabled them."* It was not limited to the apostles or to an elite group. The gift of the Spirit poured out that day transcended social, economic, and cultural boundaries. Whether Jew or Gentile, slave or free, male or female, Pentecost was for everyone gathered in the upper room. And it remains for everyone today who desires a deeper connection with God.

The Promise Of The Holy Spirit

The promise of Pentecost originates with Jesus Himself. Before His ascension, Jesus gave clear instructions to His disciples: *"Do not leave Jerusalem, but wait for the gift my Father promised, which you have heard me speak about. For John baptized with water, but in a few days, you will be baptized with the Holy Spirit."* (Acts 1:4-5). This was not merely a suggestion but a command to wait for the empowerment needed to fulfill their mission.

The baptism of the Holy Spirit was not a one-time event exclusive to the early church. In Acts 19, Paul encounters believers in Ephesus and asks, *"Did you receive the Holy Spirit when you believed?"* (Acts 19:2). When they reply that they have not even heard of the Holy Spirit, Paul lays hands on them, and they receive the Spirit, speaking in tongues and prophesying. This account demonstrates that Pentecost is a continual reality, not a historical relic. The Holy Spirit is available to all believers, across all times and places.

Pentecost is God's way of equipping His people for the work of His kingdom. Jesus Himself emphasized this when He said, *"You will receive power when the Holy Spirit comes on you; and you will be my witnesses in Jerusalem, and in all Judea and Samaria, and to the ends of the earth."* (Acts 1:8). This power is not for personal gain but for the advancement of the Gospel. It transforms ordinary believers into bold witnesses, capable of extraordinary works for the glory of God.

Revival Starts With Hunger

Revival, like Pentecost, begins with hunger. It is birthed in hearts that long for more of God, that refuse to settle for a routine faith. The upper room, where Pentecost began, was not filled with casual observers but with people united in prayer and expectation. They were willing to wait, to linger, to prioritize God's promise above all else. And because of their hunger, they experienced the outpouring of the Spirit.

Hunger for God is the catalyst for revival. It is the recognition that without Him, we are empty, powerless, and ineffective. Jesus declared in John 7:37-38, *"Let anyone who is thirsty come to Me and drink. Whoever believes in Me, as Scripture has said, rivers of living water will flow from within them."* This living water is the Holy Spirit, and it flows where there is thirst.

Imagine a church filled with hungry hearts, desperate for God's presence. Such a church would not be content with tradition or routine. It would make room for the Holy Spirit to move freely, removing blockages such as pride, control, or distractions. Revival flows through clear paths, unhindered by human resistance. It thrives in surrendered hearts that say, "Lord, have Your way."

The Outpouring At Cornelius' House: The Universality Of Pentecost

The story of Cornelius in Acts 10 is a powerful demonstration that Pentecost truly is for everyone. Cornelius, a Roman centurion, was described as a devout man who feared God, gave generously to the poor, and prayed continually. Although he was not Jewish, his reverence for God caught heaven's attention. One day, an angel appeared to him, instructing him to send for Peter, who was staying in Joppa. At the same time, God prepared Peter's heart through a vision, teaching him not to call unclean what God had made clean.

When Peter arrived at Cornelius' house, he found a large gathering of Gentiles eagerly awaiting his words. Peter began to preach about Jesus, proclaiming the good news of salvation and forgiveness of sins through Christ. As Peter spoke, the Holy Spirit fell on all who were listening. The Jewish believers who had come with Peter were astonished, because the gift of the Holy Spirit had been poured out even on the Gentiles. They heard them speaking in tongues and praising God, just as the apostles had experienced at Pentecost (Acts 10:44-46).

A lesson in God's inclusivity

The outpouring of the Holy Spirit at Cornelius' house is a reminder that Pentecost was never meant to be exclusive. The same Spirit that descended in the upper room in Jerusalem was now being poured out on Gentiles in a Roman centurion's home. This event shattered the cultural and religious barriers of the time, emphasizing that the Holy Spirit is God's gift to all who believe, regardless of their background.

Peter's words encapsulate the heart of this lesson: *"I now realize how true it is that God does not show favoritism but accepts from every nation the one who fears Him and does what is right."* (Acts 10:34-35). The baptism of the Holy Spirit is not reserved for a specific group of people, denomination, or ethnicity. It is for everyone who seeks God with a sincere heart.

Cornelius' story also highlights the importance of obedience and expectation in receiving the Holy Spirit. Cornelius acted immediately upon the angel's instructions, sending for Peter without hesitation. Similarly, Peter obeyed the Spirit's prompting to go to Cornelius, despite his initial hesitation due to cultural and religious norms. Both men positioned themselves for a divine encounter through their obedience.

This story teaches us that revival and the outpouring of the Holy Spirit often come to those who are actively seeking and expecting God to move. Cornelius and his household were gathered together, waiting to hear the Word of God. Their hunger created an atmosphere where the Spirit could move freely, resulting in a powerful outpouring.

The Power Of Testimony

Another significant aspect of this story is the role of testimony. Cornelius shared his vision and invited his household and friends to hear Peter's message. Similarly, Peter testified about Jesus' life, death, and resurrection. The testimony of both men created a bridge for the Holy Spirit to move. This demonstrates the power of sharing our faith and creating opportunities for others to encounter God.

As believers, we are called to carry the fire of Pentecost into the world. Just as Peter boldly proclaimed the Gospel to Cornelius' household, we must share the message of Jesus with those who have not yet experienced the Holy Spirit. Revival begins when we open our mouths and share the good news, trusting that the Spirit will do the rest.

The story of Cornelius challenges us to examine our own hearts. Are we creating space for the Holy Spirit to move in our lives? Are we willing to break down barriers and step outside our comfort zones to share the Gospel? Are we hungry and expectant, like Cornelius and his household, for a fresh outpouring of God's Spirit?

Pentecost is not a one-time event; it is a continual invitation to live Spirit-filled lives. The same Spirit that fell on Cornelius' house is available to us today. All we need to do is seek, surrender, and say yes to God's promise. As Jesus said, *"If you then, though you are evil, know how to give good gifts to your children, how much more will your Father in heaven give the Holy Spirit to those who ask Him!"* (Luke 11:13).

Cornelius' story reminds us that Pentecost is for everyone—Jew and Gentile, young and old, men and women. It is a gift that empowers us to live fully alive in Christ, bringing the light of the Gospel to a world in need. Let us, like Cornelius, open our hearts and homes to the Holy Spirit, creating space for revival to break out wherever we are.

The New Wineskin Of Revival

Jesus taught an essential principle about revival when He said, *"No one pours new wine into old wineskins. Otherwise, the new wine will burst the skins; the wine will run out, and the wineskins will be ruined. No, new wine must be poured into new wineskins."* (Luke 5:37-38). The new wine represents the fresh move of the Holy Spirit, and the wineskins represent the structures and attitudes needed to contain it.

Revival often exposes our inflexibility. It challenges our comfort zones and demands that we embrace change. Old habits, mindsets, and traditions that once served us well may no longer suffice for what God wants to do now. The Holy Spirit is dynamic, always moving, always creating. To resist His flow is to risk missing out on the new thing God is doing.

Are we willing to become new wineskins? Are we ready to be stretched, to let go of control, and to make room for the Spirit to move in unexpected ways? Revival is costly, but it is never unaffordable for those who are hungry for God. The question is not whether the Spirit is willing to pour out His presence; the question is whether we are prepared to receive it.

The River Of God

The Holy Spirit is often described as a river, flowing from the throne of God to bring life wherever it goes. In Ezekiel 47, the prophet sees a vision of a river flowing from the temple. As the river flows, it transforms everything it touches. Dry and barren lands become lush and fertile. Dead seas come alive. This is the power of the Holy Spirit, to bring life, healing, and transformation.

The river of God flows where it is welcomed. Like water, it seeks the path of least resistance. If our lives are filled with pride, distractions, or a desire for control, we may block the flow of the Spirit. But when we surrender, when we create a clear path, the river flows freely, bringing revival and renewal.

John 7:38-39 echoes this imagery: *"Whoever believes in Me, as Scripture has said, rivers of living water will flow from within them."* This promise is not limited to a select few. It is for every believer who is willing to yield to the Spirit. The river of God is meant to flow through us, bringing life to our families, our communities, and the world.

Pentecost: A Call To Surrender

Pentecost is not just an event to be remembered; it is a call to live surrendered lives. It invites us to yield completely to the Holy Spirit, allowing Him to lead, empower, and transform us. Surrender is not a one-time act but a daily decision to place God's will above our own.

The disciples in the upper room modeled this surrender. They waited, prayed, and obeyed Jesus' command to stay in Jerusalem until the Spirit came. Their obedience created the conditions for the outpouring of the Spirit. Likewise, our surrender creates the space for God to move in our lives. It positions us to receive His power and to walk in the fullness of His purpose.

Revival Is For Today

The same Spirit that was poured out at Pentecost is available to us today. The same power that transformed the early church can transform our lives, our churches, and our communities. Revival is not a distant dream but a present reality for those who hunger and thirst for God.

As we reflect on the significance of Pentecost, let it inspire us to seek more of the Holy Spirit. Let us clear the path, remove the blockages, and make room for God to move. Let us become vessels of His love, power, and revival to a world in desperate need of Him.

The invitation of Pentecost is for everyone. Will you accept it? Will you surrender, wait, and allow the Spirit to fill you afresh? The world needs revival, and revival begins with us. May we live as Spirit-filled believers, fully alive, fully surrendered, and fully empowered to carry the Gospel to the ends of the earth.

11

Conclusion: Revival Is Waiting For You

Revival is not some distant, elusive event reserved for the select few. It is a personal invitation from God to experience His transformative power and manifest presence. But this invitation comes with conditions; surrender, repentance, and a willingness to abandon complacency. Revival is not for the half-hearted or the lukewarm; it is for those who hunger for God with their entire being!

The scriptures remind us that revival begins in the heart. The psalmist asks, *"Who may ascend the hill of the Lord? Who may stand in His holy place? The one who has clean hands and a pure heart."* (Psalm 24:3-4). Revival cannot coexist with sin or apathy. It requires purity, dedication, and a willingness to be refined by God's holy fire.

Revival Begins With Surrender

At the core of every revival is surrender. This is not a passive giving up but an active relinquishing of control. Surrender means laying down your will, desires, and comforts to fully embrace God's plan. In Luke 9:23, Jesus says, *"Whoever wants to be my disciple must deny themselves and take up their cross daily and follow me."* Revival cannot thrive in hearts that are cluttered with self-interest. It requires a daily commitment to place God above all else.

The disciples in the upper room modeled this kind of surrender. They obeyed Jesus' command to wait for the Holy Spirit, even when they didn't fully understand what they were waiting for. Their obedience positioned them to receive the outpouring of the Holy Spirit, birthing the church and igniting a movement that changed the world.

For us today, surrender may mean giving up time, habits, or relationships that hinder our walk with God. It may mean letting go of pride, control, or comfort to allow God to have His way in our lives. True revival begins when we declare, as Jesus did in the garden, *"Not my will, but yours be done."* (Luke 22:42).

Hunger And Thirst: The Keys To Revival

Revival is not hard to find, but it requires a desperate hunger and thirst for God. Jesus promises, *"Blessed are those who hunger and thirst for righteousness, for they will be filled."* (Matthew 5:6). Revival flourishes in hearts that are unsatisfied with the status quo and yearn for a deeper encounter with God.

Hunger and thirst are powerful metaphors. They speak of urgency, necessity, and an unwillingness to settle for less. In Exodus 33:15-16, Moses expressed this hunger when he said to God, *"If your Presence does not go with us, do not send us up from here."* Moses understood that without God's presence, nothing else mattered. This same desperation is the foundation of revival.

Revival is not found in programs, traditions, or human efforts. It is birthed in the secret place, where individuals cry out to God with unrelenting passion. It is sustained by a community that collectively says, "We want more of You, Lord, no matter the cost."

Revival Lingers Where God Is Welcomed

Revival does not come and go randomly; it lingers where people make room for God. In the story of Jacob, we see an example of someone who refused to let go until he encountered God fully. After wrestling with an angel all night, Jacob declared, *"I will not let you go unless you bless me."* (Genesis 32:26). This persistence transformed Jacob's life and destiny.

Similarly, revival lingers where believers refuse to let go of God's presence. It thrives in churches, homes, and hearts where people prioritize prayer, worship, and the Word over entertainment, comfort, or routine. Revival requires believers to clear the path, removing anything that might hinder the flow of the Holy Spirit.

The Samaritan revival in John 4 is a perfect illustration. The people of Sychar begged Jesus to stay with them, and He remained for two days, during which many more came to believe. Revival lingered because the people lingered. They valued Jesus' presence above their schedules, routines, and traditions.

The Cost Of Revival

Remember that revival is costly, but it is never unaffordable. It requires repentance, humility, and a willingness to let go of sin and self-reliance. King David understood this when he said, *"I will not sacrifice to the Lord my God burnt offerings that cost me nothing."* (2 Samuel 24:24). Revival demands everything but gives infinitely more in return.

The cost of revival is not just personal; it is communal. It requires unity, sacrifice, and a collective commitment to seek God together. In Acts 2, the early church experienced revival because they were in one accord, devoting themselves to prayer, fellowship, and breaking bread together. Revival flourishes in communities where believers are willing to lay down their differences and unite under the banner of Christ.

Conclusion: Revival Is Waiting for You

The presence of God is transformative. When revival comes, it changes lives, families, churches, and communities. Isaiah 61:3 describes how God exchanges ashes for beauty, mourning for joy, and despair for praise. This is the power of revival: it takes what is broken and makes it whole.

In the Welsh Revival of 1904, entire towns were transformed by the power of God. Bars shut down, crime rates plummeted, and communities were united in worship and prayer. This revival was not the result of human effort but a sovereign move of God in response to hunger, repentance, and prayer.

The same power is available to us today. Revival brings healing to relationships, restoration to families, and renewal to churches. It ignites a passion for the lost, a commitment to holiness, and a desire to see God's kingdom come on earth as it is in heaven.

Waiting on God is an active pursuit of His presence. The disciples in the upper room did not sit around doing nothing while they waited for the Holy Spirit. They prayed, worshiped, and prepared their hearts for what was to come. Their waiting was marked by faith, expectation, and obedience.

In Isaiah 40:31(NKJV), we are reminded, *"Those who wait on the Lord shall renew their strength; they shall mount up with wings like eagles, they shall run and not be weary, they shall walk and not faint."* Waiting on God is a time of renewal and preparation. It positions us to receive His power and walk in His purposes.

As we wait for revival, we must engage in worship, prayer, and the Word. We must cultivate a lifestyle of intimacy with God, allowing Him to shape us into vessels ready to carry His fire.

Revival Is Here And Now

Revival is here and now for those who truly desire it. God is not holding back revival; He is waiting for us to step into it. The question is not whether God will move but whether we are willing to move with Him.

In Revelation 3:20, Jesus says, *"Here I am! I stand at the door and knock. If anyone hears my voice and opens the door, I will come in and eat with that person, and they with me."* Revival is as simple as opening the door to Jesus, welcoming Him into every area of our lives, and allowing Him to reign fully.

Revival Is Waiting For You

The fire of revival is not limited to specific times, places, or people. It is available to anyone who is willing to seek God wholeheartedly, surrender everything, and align their life with His will. Revival is waiting for you to say yes to God's invitation, to prioritize His presence, and to walk in the fullness of His Spirit.

Do not put out the Spirit's fire. Fan it into flame. Live with hunger, expectation, and surrender, knowing that revival is not a distant hope but a present reality for those who are willing to embrace it. Let the words of Isaiah be your prayer: "Here am I. Send me!" (Isaiah 6:8).

Revival is waiting for you. Are you ready to step into it today?

www.ingramcontent.com/pod-product-compliance
Lightning Source LLC
Chambersburg PA
CBHW061209070526
44583CB00025B/3182